S0-BFE-323

Reproducible Activities

After School
Reading Activities

Grade 4

Published by Instructional Fair • TS Denison
an imprint of

 Children's Publishing

Editors: Mary Rose Hassinger, Rebecca Warren

 Children's Publishing

Published by Instructional Fair • TS Denison
An imprint of McGraw-Hill Children's Publishing
Copyright © 2003 McGraw-Hill Children's Publishing

Send all inquiries to:
McGraw-Hill Children's Publishing
3195 Wilson Drive NW
Grand Rapids, Michigan 49544

After School Reading Activities—grade 4
ISBN: 0-7424-1774-3

1 2 3 4 5 6 7 8 9 PHXBK 08 07 06 05 04 03

Table of Contents

General Introduction

The *After School Reading Activities* series provides a unique collection of reproducible activities specifically designed for practicing key reading skills in a less formal format. Exercises provide a variety of learning experiences that inspire creativity while encouraging reading comprehension and writing practice. *After School Reading Activities* features worksheets as well as hands-on activities that present opportunities for students with different learning styles to benefit from the contents. The activities are designed for individuals, pairs of students, or small groups to use.

Standards Mastery
Although this series is meant to provide practice in a non-threatening format, activities support many of the NCTE/IRA standards. Experience with several genres of writing (including fiction and nonfiction) is included within each skill area. Activities demand that a variety of strategies be used in order to complete the work. Examples of strategies are using prior knowledge, using word identification, and using graphics. Students will be asked to evaluate and synthesize information and then to communicate it in a variety of ways, from writing brief sentences, to filling in a story map, to creating pictures, and to participating in group activities.

Organization
The book is arranged in skill areas as follows:

 Word Skills
- Arranged in a progressive, sequential format
- Digraphs, blends, root words, and more

 Vocabulary Development
- High-interest and high-frequency words, including reproducible pages to make flash cards
- Cross-curricular (science, social studies, and math)

 Reading Comprehension
- One- and two-page articles
- Story elements, inferencing, following directions, and more

Use
As you prepare to make this series a part of an activity schedule, have the following items on hand:

Crayons	Stapler	Scissors
Markers	Brads	Glue
Construction paper	Hole punch	Library books
Tagboard	Pencils	Reference materials

General Introduction (cont.)

Structure

Plan to use the reproducible pages in centers, for independent practice, or with small groups of students. Photocopy the pages of flash cards, and devote time to having the students make the flash cards for future use. Reproduce the selected pages to provide a variety of activities designed to ensure increased achievement while having fun.

Extension Activities

The format of many of the activities make them ideal for adapting the type of exercise to other materials. Some ideas are

Choose a popular poem or a familiar passage from a story and have students circle a given letter or digraph sound or word from a specified origin. Take the opportunity to expose the student to various types of print such as newspapers, magazines, and brochures. Focus on the content vocabulary being taught in class and progress into the more difficult concepts.

Have students write or dictate their own word riddles, using vocabulary from a lesson that they are currently studying. Have students use pictures and drawings in the riddles as well as words and sentences.

The sets of flash cards have many uses, such as

The flash cards are printed back-to-back and so can be removed from the book, colored, laminated, and reused. They can also be reproduced so that each student has his own set. Use the cards to increase meaning vocabulary in the theme they are based upon. The words can be used in a self-checking quiz situation, or partners can quiz each other. Have students reveal either the word or the definition and then give the other side. Students should be able to master the words either way.

The sets of flash cards can be used individually or together. One way would be to have students choose two cards from each theme and use them in an oral story. Another would be to sort the words by category or theme, by syllables, or by beginning sounds.

The flash cards can also be used as the required vocabulary for class books in certain themes.

Name _____ Date _____

In Patriotic Order

Number each group of patriotic words in alphabetical order. Then write the first letter of the number-two word in the matching blank below. The first two are done for you.

1. _*2_ enemy
   _1_ eagle
   _3_ forge

2. _*2_ Marines
   _3_ party
   _1_ main

3. ____ united
   ____ weak
   ____ weapons

4. ____ honor
   ____ infantry
   ____ honest

5. ____ defend
   ____ grave
   ____ dedication

6. ____ parade
   ____ Marine
   ____ parody

7. ____ glory
   ____ headstone
   ____ heard

8. ____ annual
   ____ amnesty
   ____ American

9. ____ monuments
   ____ memorial
   ____ open

10. ____ Uncle
    ____ treaty
    ____ Sam

11. ____ valor
    ____ tactics
    ____ veterans

12. ____ yearn
    ____ Yankee
    ____ violent

13. ____ yesterday
    ____ peace
    ____ youth

14. ____ religion
    ____ respect
    ____ soldier

15. ____ stars
    ____ yesteryear
    ____ youth

16. ____ salute
    ____ taps
    ____ tribute

17. ____ gravestone
    ____ nation
    ____ loyality

18. ____ armed forces
    ____ attack
    ____ freedom

19. ____ battle
    ____ enthusiasm
    ____ glory

20. ____ bugle
    ____ Arlington Cemetery
    ____ air raid

21. ____ tactics
    ____ honor
    ____ induction

22. ____ army
    ____ anger
    ____ bold

23. ____ forgive
    ____ educate
    ____ bravery

24. ____ epitaph
    ____ ceremony
    ____ flag

25. ____ dedicate
    ____ decorations
    ____ flowers

26. ____ peace
    ____ create
    ____ offer

E
‾10‾ ‾4‾ ‾24‾ ‾15‾ ‾6‾ ‾20‾ ‾11‾ ‾1‾ ‾25‾ ‾16‾ ‾7‾ ‾23‾ ‾3‾ ‾18‾ ‾12‾

For
M
‾9‾ ‾19‾ ‾2‾ ‾26‾ ‾14‾ ‾21‾ ‾8‾ ‾17‾ ‾5‾ ‾22‾ ‾13‾

Name _____ Date _____

Guide-Worthy Words

Write ten vocabulary words from the Word Bank under each of the guide word pairs. Remember to write them in alphabetical order.

1.

Reflection	Syllable

2.

Abrupt	Authority

3.

Babyhood	Crest

4.

Defense	Exult

Word Bank

burrow	commence	cordial	corporal	accustom
accidentally	barracks	barometer	explosive	schoolmaster
stealth	allow	calamity	stance	defiant
epidemic	ancient	scowl	discard	ammunition
disturbance	subside	salute	reindeer	consternation
assign	demoralize	disposition	appoint	beneficial
resolute	enormous	ashamed	retort	entirely
earthenware	additional	commotion	almanac	surpass

Name _____ Date _____

Cloudy Skies

Write the plural form of the word on the line below each cloud.
On a separate sheet use five of the new words in sentences.

1.  party

2.  dish

3.  beach

_____   _____   _____

4.  ditch

5.  stick

6.  lunch

_____   _____   _____

7.  crutch

8.  piece

9.  store

_____   _____   _____

10.  daisy

11.  cartoon

12.  doll

_____   _____   _____

13.  tree

14.  cherry

15.  sky

_____   _____   _____

Name _____ Date _____

Two Vowels Go Walking

Fill in the blanks with the missing vowels. Use **ai**, **ay**, **ea**, **ee**, **oa**, **oe**, or **ue**.

1. gl ____ ____

2. f ____ ____ st

3. x-r ____ ____

4. t ____ ____ st

5. ch ____ ____ n

6. n ____ ____ dle

7. t ____ ____ s

8. h ____ ____ stack

9. p ____ ____ nut

10. t ____ ____

11. s ____ ____ p

12. t ____ ____ l

13. g ____ ____ t

14. p ____ ____

15. ch ____ ____ se

16. sn ____ ____ l

17. t ____ ____ th

18. spr ____ ____

0-7424-1774-3 *After School Reading Activities*

What's That Noise?

Use the words from the Word Bank to complete the crossword puzzle.

Across

5. trip at sea
6. harmful substance
7. to express joy
9. to take pleasure from
11. an agreement to meet
13. faithfulness
15. sound produced by speaking

Down

1. to bring together
2. to stay away from
3. to ruin
4. farm crop
8. one who pays wages
10. dampness
12. selection
14. regal

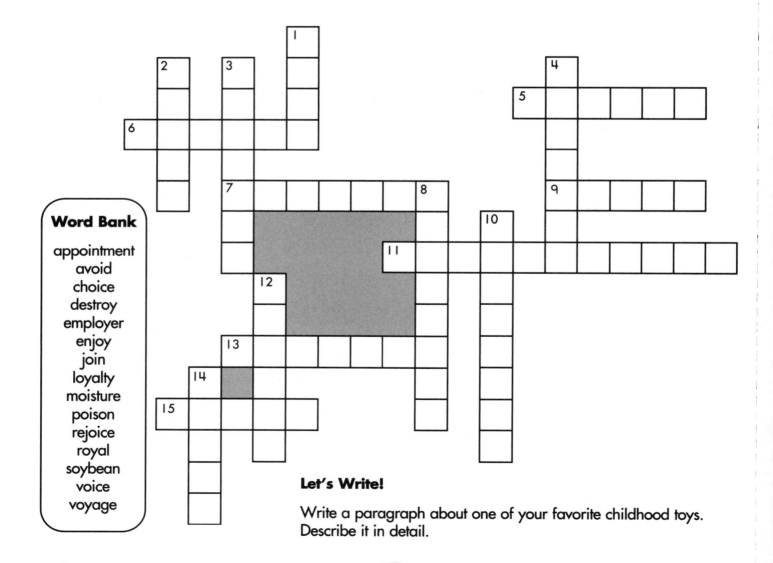

Word Bank

appointment
avoid
choice
destroy
employer
enjoy
join
loyalty
moisture
poison
rejoice
royal
soybean
voice
voyage

Let's Write!

Write a paragraph about one of your favorite childhood toys. Describe it in detail.

Name _____ Date _____

Sweet Syllables

Count the number of syllables in each word. Write the number in the blank.

1. pineapple _____

2. Africa _____

3. skate _____

4. dress _____

5. pizza _____

6. flash _____

7. apple _____

8. magic _____

9. Olympic _____

10. sesame _____

11. hamburger _____

12. supper _____

13. magnify _____

14. Samantha _____

15. restaurant _____

0-7424-1774-3 *After School Reading Activities*

The Root of the Matter

Look at each root word and its meaning. Write the word from the Word Bank that contains the root word.

Root	Meaning	New Word
1. aqua	water	_____
2. port	carry	_____
3. voc	voice	_____
4. bio	life	_____
5. dent	tooth	_____
6. phon	sound	_____
7. ped	foot	_____
8. dorm	sleep	_____

Word Bank

biography   phonics   vocalist
dentist   centipede portable
aquarium   dormitory

Across
1—man-made home for sea life
2—the study of language sounds
3—living arrangement for students
4—able to be carried

Down
5—an expert in tooth care
6—story of someone's life
7—someone who can sing
8—hundred-footed

Name _____ Date _____

Break It Up!

For each word given below, give the base word and the prefix and/or suffix. Remember, the spelling of some base words changes when adding suffixes. Not all words have a prefix and a suffix.

Word	Prefix	Base Word	Suffix
1. resourceful			
2. accomplishment			
3. numbness			
4. convincing			
5. merciless			
6. sturdiest			
7. disobeying			
8. unmistakable			
9. disinfecting			
10. disclaimed			
11. reopening			
12. inventive			
13. restless			
14. precaution			
15. imitating			

Name _____ Date _____

Let It Snow

Mark the vowels in each word long or short. Then, color the snowflakes containing long vowels blue. Color the snowflakes containing short vowels red.

1. puddle

2. beach

3. bright

4. stake

5. mail

6. platter

7. globe

8. punch

9. nuzzle

10. socks

11. sealed

12. swine

13. splatter

14. thrive

15. risen

16. kettle

17. fresh

18. bucket

19. plant

20. trick

Name _____ Date _____

"R" Takes Charge

Fill in the blanks of each word with **ar**, **er**, **ir**, **or**, or **ur** to make a word that matches the picture.

 1. t _____ _____ get

 **2.** _____ _____ ange

 3. b _____ _____ d

 **4.** t _____ _____ tle

 **5.** st _____ _____

 6. n _____ _____ se

 7. hamm _____ _____

 **8.** b _____ _____ n

 **9.** sk _____ _____ t

 **10.** st _____ _____ k

 **11.** c _____ _____ ls

 **12.** g _____ _____ den

 **13.** h _____ _____ se

 **14.** feath _____ _____

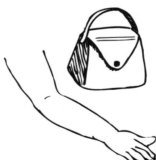 **15.** p _____ _____ se

 **16.** _____ _____ m

 **17.** c _____ _____ cle

18. g _____ _____ affe

0-7424-1774-3 *After School Reading Activities*

Slippery Blasts

Read the poems. Circle the words that begin with the blend **bl** or **sl**.

Blizzard blowing
On our block!
Blow! Blow!
Blankets of snow,
Blasts of snow!

Never sleep on a sled!
Never sleep on a sled!
You'll slip and slide,
It's a slippery ride!
No, never sleep on a sled!

Read the clues. Use the poem to find missing **bl** and **sl** words.
Write them in the puzzle.

Across

3. Listen to the wind _____ !

5. We have new _____ on our beds.

6. Let's go to the playground and play on the _____ .

7. Don't _____ on the wet floor!

8. The icy roads are _____ .

Down

1. We live one _____ from school.

2. School was let out early because of the big _____ .

3. I felt _____ of cold air whenever someone opened the door.

6. It is fun to _____ out in a tent.

7. Max likes to _____ down the snowy hills.

Name _____ Date _____

Enough!

Write the digraph **gh** on the lines to complete the words in the poem. Read the poem.

Cou _____ enou _____

And it feels rou _____ !

Lau _____ enou _____

And life won't feel tou _____ !

Use the poem as a Word Bank. Find the **gh** words to complete the sentences.

1. We need to sand this board because it is too _____ .

2. The clown made us all _____ .

3. Our steak was too _____ to cut.

4. Our class earned _____ money to go on a field trip.

5. The smoke from the campfire made us all _____ .

Write a rhyming poem about something that makes you laugh.

_____

_____

_____

_____

Draw a picture to go with your poem.

All the Way to the End

Add a suffix to each word in parentheses to make a new word that makes sense in the sentence. Write the word in the blank.

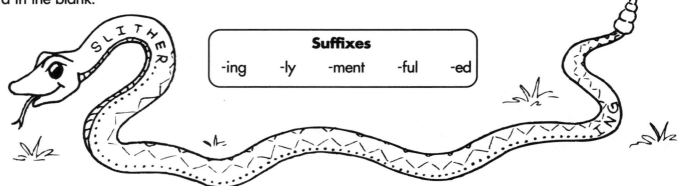

Suffixes				
-ing	-ly	-ment	-ful	-ed

1. No _____ is allowed during our science test.
        (talk)

2. Maggie _____ repotted the house plants.
        (tender)

3. Everyone felt _____ that the warm weather was coming soon.
        (hope)

4. Both children placed their _____ clothes in the dresser.
        (fold)

5. The family plays ping-pong in the _____ .
        (base)

6. Max was _____ and couldn't concentrate on his math _____ .
        (rest)   (assign)

7. He seemed to work _____ to build the cabin.
        (endless)

8. It was a big _____ when rain fell on the parade.
        (disappoint)

9. The small children _____ to be airplanes.
        (pretend)

10. A fire was _____ in the fireplace.
        (blaze)

11. Mom and Dad _____ read the newspaper together.
        (usual)

12. My birthday party was a _____ surprise.
        (wonder)

This Suffix Is Terrific

The Greek suffix **–ic** has several meanings: having to do with; consisting or containing; produced by; like; and a person or thing belonging to.

Complete each sentence with the correct word from the Word Bank.

Word Bank			
symphonic	romantic	terrific	scenic
volcanic	photographic	scientific	majestic
angelic	nomadic	democratic	sporadic

1. The rains were so _____ that the crops failed.

2. We took the _____ route along the river bluffs.

3. There is _____ evidence that smoking cigarettes is hazardous to your health.

4. The show was so _____ that we went to see it again.

5. The _____ ash from Mt. St. Helens blanketed a huge area.

6. Dad prefers _____ music to rock and roll.

7. Jan has a lot of _____ equipment in his darkroom.

8. _____ people have no permanent homes.

9. Giving your sweetheart flowers is a _____ thing to do.

10. Many countries in the world have a _____ form of government.

11. The sleeping baby looked _____ in his mother's arms.

12. The lion, the king of beasts, looked _____ as he stood in the twilight.

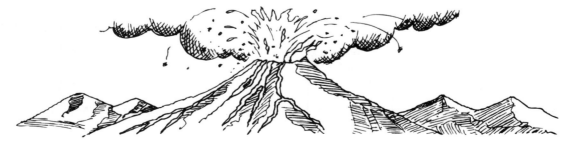

Name _____ Date _____

Fanciful Hats

Add a suffix to each base word. Write it on the line.

Suffixes				
-ing	-ly	-less	-ful	-er

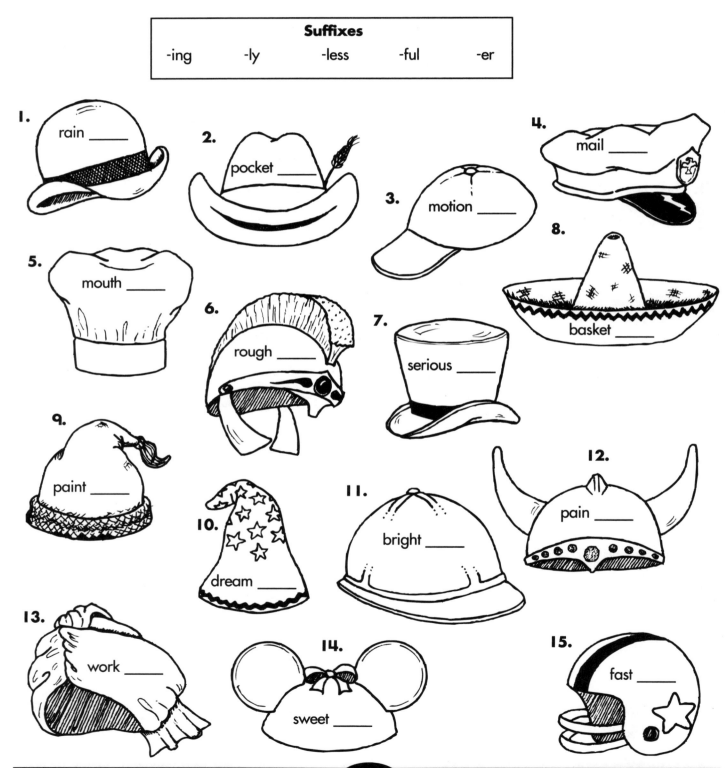

1. rain _____

2. pocket _____

3. motion _____

4. mail _____

5. mouth _____

6. rough _____

7. serious _____

8. basket _____

9. paint _____

10. dream _____

11. bright _____

12. pain _____

13. work _____

14. sweet _____

15. fast _____

Prefixes

Name _____ Date _____

Number Words

Use the Word Bank to complete the crossword puzzle.

Word Bank

bicycle
bifocals
bimonthly
binoculars
quadrangle
quadruplet
triangle
tricep
tricorn
tricycle
trio
tripod
unicorn
unicycle
uniform

Across

2. three-sided figure
4. mythical horse with one horn
6. rectangular area with buildings on four sides
7. eyeglasses having two focal lengths
8. three-wheeler
12. every two months
13. three-cornered hat in early times

Down

1. field glasses
2. group of three musicians
3. two-wheeler
5. three-legged camera support
6. one of four babies born at a single birth
9. one-wheeler
10. all the same
11. arm muscle with three points of origin

Let's Write

Divide a sheet of paper. List advantages and disadvantages of being a twin, a triplet, or one of a set of quadruplets.

 0-7424-1774-3 *After School Reading Activities*

Prefixes

Name _____ Date _____

Don't Miss This

The prefix **mis-** means wrongly; bad or badly; no or not. Look at the puzzle. Circle the base words of the following words. They may be horizontal, diagonal, or vertical.

misadventure
misapply
misbehave
miscall
miscast
mischance
misconduct
miscount
misdeal
misdeed
misdirect
misfile
misfire

misfit
misfortune
misgovern
misguide
mishandle
mishear
mislay
mislead
misname
misplay
misread
misrule

S	F	A	P	P	L	Y	G	F	R	E
A	I	O	D	E	A	L	I	N	E	L
T	L	E	C	V	O	R	E	M	A	U
L	E	V	A	H	E	B	A	Y	D	R
D	E	P	L	A	Y	N	S	T	I	F
I	L	A	L	C	A	S	T	C	R	M
R	D	S	D	L	E	D	I	U	G	T
E	N	U	T	R	O	F	S	D	R	H
C	A	O	H	M	C	H	A	N	C	E
T	H	B	L	K	T	N	U	O	C	A
G	O	V	E	R	N	T	N	C	O	R

Choose a word from the list above. Complete the sentences.

1. Jeremy is _____ in the play—he should have been the villain.

2. Did I _____ the car keys?

3. It was my _____ to be the first called on in class.

4. I think I saw you _____ the cards.

5. Did the cannon _____ ?

6. Our vacation turned out to be one _____ after another.

7. Don't _____ that crystal vase or you might break it.

8. I think I _____ that paragraph—I didn't understand it at all.

9. Robbing a bank is a _____ .

10. Following wrong directions will _____ you.

Name _____ Date _____

'Tis the Season

Some words have more than one meaning. Carefully read the different meanings for each word below. Then write a letter in the blank to show how the word is used in each sentence.

season: **a.** one of the four divisions of the year
b. the time when something takes place
c. add spices to

_____ **1.** Spring is my favorite **season**.

_____ **2.** We go to many baseball games during the **season**.

_____ **3.** **Season** the potatoes with salt and pepper.

beam: **a.** smile warmly
b. ray of light
c. thick piece of wood

_____ **4.** I saw Josie **beam** when she received the trophy.

_____ **5.** The **beam** from the flashlight fell on the floor.

_____ **6.** I hope that **beam** doesn't fall on us.

pick: **a.** eat sparingly
b. open with a wire
c. provoke

_____ **7.** Please don't **pick** a fight with Carlos.

_____ **8.** Don't **pick** at your green beans.

_____ **9.** Dad will have to **pick** the lock because he forgot his keys.

select: **a.** excellent
b. hand-picked
c. choose

_____ **10.** She was chosen from a **select** group.

_____ **11.** Which pictures are you going to **select**?

_____ **12.** These fresh strawberries are **select**.

Borrowed from Abroad

Many words in the English language come from other languages. For example, *garage* comes from a French word meaning *protect*.

Use a dictionary to find the language from which each of the following words was taken. Write the name of the language and a short definition for each.

1. gimlet: _____

_____

2. hacienda: _____

_____

3. javelin: _____

_____

4. jerky: _____

_____

5. morgue: _____

6. terrazzo: _____

_____

Answer the following questions.

7. Which two words from above are from Spanish?

_____

8. Which two words have a French origin?

_____

9. Which word is the name of something to eat?

_____

10. Where would you likely find terrazzo—in a morgue or a hacienda?

_____

Name _____ Date _____

Similar in Some Way

Put an **X** in the circle by the phrase to correctly complete each analogy.

1. conductor is to orchestra as . . .	○ scene is to actor ○ director is to play
2. absent is to present as . . .	○ adult is to child ○ levy is to tax
3. button is to blouse as . . .	○ coat is to hat ○ zipper is to skirt
4. pork is to hog as . . .	○ bacon is to eggs ○ beef is to cattle
5. allow is to permit as . . .	○ alter is to change ○ refute is to confirm
6. mirror is to reflect as . . .	○ scissors is to cut ○ read is to book
7. aide is to assistant as . . .	○ brash is to cautious ○ convince is to persuade
8. autumn is to season as . . .	○ winter is to summer ○ Halloween is to holiday
9. shirt is to collar as . . .	○ sock is to shoes ○ trousers is to cuffs
10. ice cream is to dessert as . . .	○ cereal is to breakfast ○ supper is to dinner
11. graph is to chart as . . .	○ present is to past ○ explore is to investigate

Name _____ Date _____

Aardvark to Zebra

Use the clues below to determine the double-letter alphabet words. Write each word in the space provided.

AA = _____ African animal

BB = _____ synonym for hare or bunny

CC = _____ masked animal with ringed tail

DD = _____ not in sight

EE = _____ fastest land animal

FF = _____ bread cooked inside a turkey

GG = _____ where a yellow yolk is found

HH = _____ to thumb a ride

II = _____ sliding down a snowy slope

LL = _____ the home of a hermit crab

MM= _____ a pounding tool

NN = _____ humorous

OO = _____ a chocolate-chip treat

PP = _____ large water mammal

RR = _____ feeling bad about something you did

SS = _____ across and down clue-type puzzle

TT = _____ a spacecraft that lands like an airplane

UU = _____ a sweeper

ZZ = _____ light rain

Name _____ Date _____

Hear! Here! for Homophones

Circle the correct homophones in each sentence.

1. I hope his (heal, heel, he'll) will (heal, heel, he'll) soon so (heal, heel, he'll) be able to resume running.

2. Mark (paste, paced) the floor while he waited for Ahmed to (paste, paced) the picture to the poster.

3. (Pleas, Please) listen to the little girl's (pleas, please) for help.

4. The (crew's, cruise) job on the (crew's, cruise) is to make passengers happy.

5. The mountain climber became (bolder, boulder) as she climbed from one (bolder, boulder) to the next.

6. You don't have to have much (muscle, mussel) to open a (muscle, mussel).

7. Can you (pare, pear) the (pare, pear) for me?

8. Roberto (peeks, peaks) out the plane's window at the snowy (peeks, peaks) below.

9. (Wait, Weight) here while I find out the (wait, weight) of the package.

10. The (colonel, kernel) could not eat just one (colonel, kernel) of popcorn.

On the lines below, write a sentence using each pair of homophones.

11. tail, tale _____

_____

12. been, bin _____

_____

13. heard, herd _____

_____

14. steal, steel _____

_____

15. fair, fare _____

_____

Name _____ Date _____

This Will Be No Contest for You

Write the correct pronunciation for each bold-faced word. Use the key below.

┌───┐
| **Pronunciations** |

content:	(k ən tent')	**desert:**	(di zurt')	**contest:**	(k ən test')
	(kän' tent)		(dez' ərt)		(kän' test)
commune:	(k ə myoon')	**escort:**	(es' kôrt)	**close:**	(clōs)
	(käm' yoon)		(i skôrt')		(clōz)
record:	(ri kord')	**refuse:**	(ref' yoos)		
	(rek' ərd)		(ri fyooz')		

1. I am not yet **content** (_____) with the **content** (_____) of my science report.

2. Don't **close** (_____) the door because the air in the room will get **close** (_____).

3. The second-place winner will **contest** (_____) the results of the **contest** (_____).

4. Did the soldier **desert** (_____) the troops out in the **desert** (_____)?

5. The band will **record** (_____) a new **record** (_____).

6. Do you think people **commune** (_____) with nature at the **commune** (_____)?

7. The trash collector will **refuse** (_____) to take any yard **refuse** (_____) not in a plastic bag.

8. Sherri's **escort** (_____) will **escort** (_____) her to the dance.

Name _____ Date _____

Your Number's Up

The words in the Word Bank all have Greek or Latin prefixes and refer to numbers.
Use the Word Bank to write the word that completes each sentence.

Word Bank

quadrupeds	trisect	unicorn	decathlon
octopus	centipede	bilingual	hexagon
decade	Pentagon	biathlon	quadrilateral
trio	centennial		

1. The five-sided government building in Washington, D.C., is called the _____.

2. I saw an _____ with eight legs at the aquarium.

3. The athletes who compete in the _____ combine cross-country skiing and marksmanship.

4. The _____ teacher spoke English and French fluently.

5. Four-footed animals are called _____.

6. A _____ is a figure with six sides and six angles.

7. Our city is one hundred years old, and we are having a gigantic _____ celebration.

8. I will _____ the figure so there will be three equal parts.

9. Do you think a _____ really has one hundred legs?

10. The _____ was composed of a violinist, a cellist, and a bass player.

11. A _____ is a mythical animal with one horn.

12. There are ten years in a _____.

13. A plane figure with four sides and four angles is called a _____.

14. Athletes competing in ten track and field events are participating in a _____.

0-7424-1774-3 *After School Reading Activities*

Name _____ Date _____

Now Try This

The prefix **tri-**, which means *having three*, comes from French, Latin, and Greek origins.

Write the correct word from the Word Bank in the blank to compete the sentence.

Word Bank		
tricentennial	triangle	triceps
tricolored	tricycle	trivet
triplicate	tripod	triple
triceratops	trident	trilogy
trifocals	triplets	trio

1. The little boy rode his new _____.

2. The French flag is _____.

3. Please set this hot dish on a _____.

4. _____ was a dinosaur with three horns.

5. The United States will celebrate its _____ in 2076.

6. Dad put the camera on a _____ before he took the picture.

7. Jose hit a _____ to get to third base.

8. Jack, Janie, and Joe are _____.

9. I think I'll need _____ to see better.

10. The gymnast has developed large _____.

11. Mr. Jones will need the report in _____.

12. The _____ sang my favorite song.

13. Have you read Sanderson's _____?

14. I can draw an isosceles _____.

15. A _____ is a three-pronged spear.

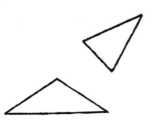

Name _____ Date _____

Forests

Across

3. making the best use of and protecting the forests, land, and other natural resources

5. a mixture of ground-up wood used for making paper

6. layers of wood glued and pressed together

8. a place where trees are grown for harvesting

9. a substance put into the soil to give extra food to plants

Down

1. a person who is employed to guard the forest

2. a pond of water near a sawmill that is used for storing logs

4. a place where logs are sawed into boards

7. a lumberjack

8. a region near the equator with rain forests

Word Bank

evergreens	fertilizer	forest ranger	logger
machete	conservation	millpond	national forest
plywood	pulp	rain forest	sawmill
tree farm	tropical	water cycle	watershed

 # Weird Words

Use a dictionary to help you answer the questions. Use complete sentences.

1. Which would you use to treat a sore throat: a **gargoyle** or a **gargle**?

_____

2. Which might be used on a gravestone: an **epiphyte** or an **epitaph**?

_____

3. Which is an instrument: **calligraphy** or a **calliope**?

_____

4. Would a building have a **gargoyle** or an **argyle** on it?

_____

5. If you trick someone, do you **bamboozle** him or **barcarole** him?

_____

6. If you studied handwriting, would you learn **calligraphy** or **cajolery**?

_____

7. What would a gondolier sing: a **barcarole** or an **argyle**?

_____

8. If you tried to coax someone, would you be using **cajolery** or **calamity**?

_____

9. Which might you wear: **argyles** or **calliopes**?

_____

10. In Venice, Italy, would you travel in a **gondola** or a **calamity**?

_____

Geographic Juggle

Unscramble and write each geographic term. Then draw a picture to illustrate the meaning of each term.

1. _____ (yalevl)	2. _____ (tiomuann)	3. _____ (oncayn)	4. _____ (noalvoc)
5. _____ (ohbrar)	6. _____ (lipan)	7. _____ (aceon)	8. _____ (tacos)
9. _____ (erirv)	10. _____ (uneplnais)	11. _____ (flug)	12. _____ (inctetonn)
13. _____ (ase)	14. _____ (tupaela)	15. _____ (daslin)	16. _____ (kale)

Name _____ Date _____

Don't Pollute

Use the words from the Word Bank to help complete the puzzle.

Across

1. the wearing away of the earth by wind, water, and ice

6. this endangers ocean life

8. the science of the relationship between living things and their environment

10. the natural, living part of the world

Down

2. energy that is sent out from atoms and molecules

3. smoke and fog

4. makes our environment dirty and unhealthy

5. to use something over and over again

7. chemicals used to control insects—they can be harmful to plants and animals

9. trash thrown about and not disposed of

Word Bank

smog	pollution	recycle	reservoir
exhaust	pesticides	litter	landfill
sanitation	conservation	environment	ecology
radiation	erosion	incinerator	oil spill

Name _____ Date _____

Birds of a Feather

Use the words from the Word Bank to build a puzzle with names of birds.
Hint: Build off the word *partridge*.

Word Bank

gull	lark	sparrow	finch	bluebird
jay	swan	goose	cuckoo	raven
dove	ostrich	quail	oriole	canary
hawk	crane	pheasant	wren	

Explain what you think each saying means.

"Birds of a feather flock together." _____

_____

"The early bird catches the worm." _____

_____

"A bird in the hand is worth two in the bush." _____

_____

Name _____ Date _____

Some Body

Unscramble each word. Use the correct color to trace the line from each word to the matching part of the body. Use the same color to write each word in the correct sentence below.

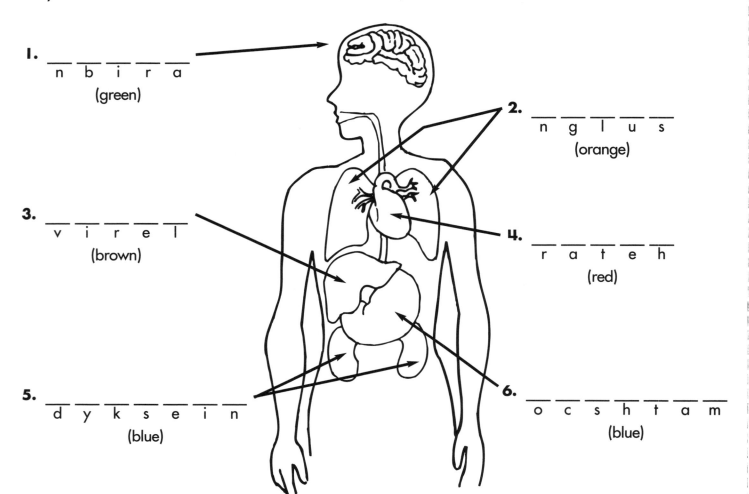

1. _ _ _ _ _
   n b i r a
   (green)

2. _ _ _ _ _ _
   n g l u s
   (orange)

3. _ _ _ _ _
   v i r e l
   (brown)

4. _ _ _ _ _ _
   r a t e h
   (red)

5. _ _ _ _ _ _ _
   d y k s e i n
   (blue)

6. _ _ _ _ _ _ _ _
   o c s h t a m
   (blue)

7. The _____ pumps blood to all parts of the body.

8. The _____ helps digest the food that is eaten.

9. The _____ are filled with air that is breathed.

10. The _____ is the thinking part of the body.

11. The _____ are helpful in keeping blood clean.

12. The _____ makes a liquid which also helps in digestion.

0-7424-1774-3 *After School Reading Activities*

Name _____ Date _____

Threatened and Endangered Animals

Use the names of the threatened and endangered animals in the Word Bank to build a puzzle.
Only use the bold-faced words. Build off the word **rhinoceros**.

Word Bank			
brown **hyena**	Darwin's **rhea**	red **wolf**	black-footed **ferret**
Spanish **lynx**	Philippine **eagle**	**gavial**	ring-tailed **lemur**
giant **panda**	blue **whale**	**numbat**	resplendent **quetzal**
Arabian **oryx**	Grevy's **zebra**	**kakapo**	Galapagos **penguin**
Indian **python**	wild **yak**	**dugong**	

Use an encyclopedia to answer the following questions.

1. Which animal above is related to the manatee? _____

2. Which is the cousin of the crocodile? _____

3. Which is related to the ostrich? _____

     0-7424-1774-3 *After School Reading Activities*

Name _____ Date _____

Ocean Motion

Search for the words from the Word Bank in the puzzle below.

B	A	C	F	S	E	A	U	R	C	H	I	N	U	M	C
S	E	O	G	E	I	N	A	X	I	N	D	I	A	N	O
E	A	N	T	A	R	C	T	I	C	P	E	O	N	I	R
A	F	T	U	W	L	C	S	R	N	T	G	C	E	S	A
H	B	I	O	E	G	I	A	V	P	I	M	E	O	T	L
O	P	N	V	E	A	L	T	W	O	D	E	A	S	A	R
R	U	E	I	D	E	T	L	A	M	A	K	N	I	R	E
S	R	N	D	A	P	L	A	V	E	L	S	O	F	F	E
E	S	T	L	V	L	C	N	O	R	W	D	G	R	I	F
Y	O	L	G	O	A	H	T	S	R	A	O	R	M	S	G
A	N	E	M	O	N	E	I	H	D	V	I	A	R	H	N
N	A	M	Y	E	K	B	C	F	L	E	S	P	T	X	E
P	R	I	T	N	T	O	H	P	A	X	Y	H	I	W	L
L	I	S	B	T	O	S	W	A	C	G	F	Y	V	Y	N
A	M	A	R	I	N	E	B	I	O	L	O	G	I	S	T
R	E	K	M	Y	A	R	H	D	K	I	C	J	S	B	O
C	U	R	R	E	N	T	S	W	O	M	T	B	K	W	A
T	L	U	G	U	L	F	S	T	R	E	A	M	I	A	C
I	H	M	D	M	E	L	K	I	P	A	C	I	F	I	C
C	E	Y	N	S	F	A	T	H	O	M	S	C	E	R	Y

Word Bank

Atlantic	Pacific	Indian	Arctic
Antarctic	currents	oceanography	continent
coral reef	seaweed	tidal wave	anemone
seahorse	sea urchin	starfish	plankton
Gulf Stream	fathoms	sonar	marine biologist

0-7424-1774-3 *After School Reading Activities*

Name _____ Date _____

Americans All

People from many different countries have come to live in the United States. They have brought with them the rich heritage and culture of their native lands.

Build a puzzle with the names of twenty-one countries from which people have emigrated to America. The letters given in the puzzle will help you.

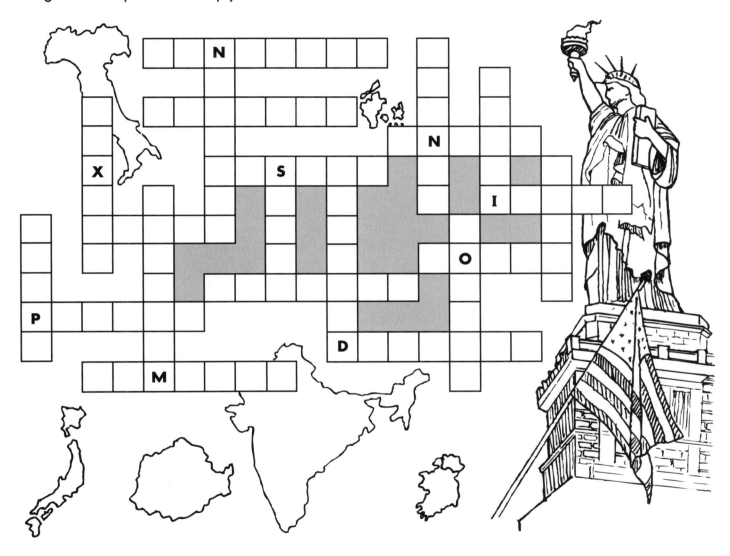

Word Bank

China	Egypt	Haiti	India	Italy
Japan	Korea	Spain	France	Mexico
Norway	Poland	Russia	Denmark	England
Ireland	Nigeria	Romania	Vietnam	Tanzania
Hungary				

Name _____ Date _____

Antonyms from A to Z

Using the words from the Word Bank, write the antonym of each clue in the puzzle.

Across

5. brutal
7. safety
8. discourage
10. inept
11. meet
12. plentiful
13. joy
18. upset
20. release
22. humble
23. somber
24. brisk
25. protect

Down

1. attract
2. stingy
3. noisy
4. attack
6. far
9. energy
14. flatter
15. ancient
16. disgrace
17. relax
19. ordinary
21. serious

Word Bank

liberal	kind	console	peril	honor
fatigue	grief	evade	insult	jolly
betray	able	meager	near	odd
defend	quiet	repel	seize	tense
young	vain	warm	urge	zany

0-7424-1774-3 *After School Reading Activities*

Name _____ Date _____

Football Fame Frames

Circle the football words found in the puzzle below. They are horizontal, vertical, and diagonal.

T	Y	A	R	D	L	I	N	E	R	E	T	N	E	C	P	Q	B	U	I	W	C
V	K	C	A	E	I	E	L	D	D	U	H	E	L	M	E	T	L	N	T	I	L
K	C	O	F	F	E	N	S	E	A	K	P	E	M	N	V	S	O	W	N	D	I
C	A	A	D	E	K	P	I	B	G	O	A	L	P	O	S	T	C	O	O	E	P
A	B	C	O	N	C	P	D	I	Z	T	E	A	M	W	O	R	K	D	I	R	P
B	R	H	O	S	M	I	E	L	S	O	V	U	P	L	K	T	C	H	T	E	I
G	E	C	B	E	N	G	L	C	Q	T	I	S	L	M	I	A	G	C	P	C	N
N	T	E	O	F	F	S	I	D	E	D	S	A	T	Y	T	I	U	U	E	E	G
I	R	E	W	E	T	K	N	X	A	A	B	K	U	E	N	L	A	O	C	I	Y
N	A	R	L	J	X	I	E	T	P	T	J	C	O	S	U	B	R	T	R	V	T
N	U	E	M	S	R	N	S	H	O	U	L	D	E	R	P	A	D	S	E	E	L
U	Q	F	I	E	L	D	G	O	A	L	T	O	M	E	I	C	B	U	T	R	A
R	O	E	F	T	P	F	F	O	K	C	I	K	I	J	M	K	I	P	N	I	N
S	C	R	I	M	M	A	G	E	M	V	I	C	T	O	R	Y	C	E	I	P	E
S	K	O	O	B	Y	A	L	P	G	R	I	D	I	R	O	N	L	R	Q	V	P

Answer This

There are two more hidden words that describe the championship game all pro football players aim for. Find them and list here:

_____ _____

Word Bank

pass	center	guard
punt	scrimmage	defense
helmet	clipping	offense
stadium	sidelines	offside
field goal	yard line	kickoff
referee	goal post	timeout
coach	gridiron	playbook
penalty	wide receiver	teamwork
running back	touchdown	pigskin
jersey	huddle	cleats
football	shoulder pads	block
quarterback	interception	
tailback	victory	

Name _____ Date _____

Medieval March

Use the words from the Word Bank to complete the puzzle. Use a dictionary or encyclopedia if necessary.

Across
1. customs of medieval knighthood
2. King Arthur's sword
3. King Arthur's circular table
5. combat on horseback
6. magician of King Arthur's court
7. steel-tipped spear of knights
8. water-filled trench around a castle
9. a feudal tenant
10. a knightly martial sport

Down
1. armor bearer for a knight
2. a young boy who wants to be a knight
3. the church seat of a bishop
4. a successful squire becomes one
5. metallic body covering
6. an establishment for monks
7. a medieval brother
8. a symbolic emblem
9. a large, fortified building

Word Bank

moat	vassal	tournament	knight
coat of arms	Excalibur	friar	monastery
round table	armor	joust	castle
squire	chivalry	cathedral	
lance	page	Merlin	

Name _____ Date _____

Words We Can Hear

Words that imitate the sounds that they are associated with are onomatopoeic. Use words from the Word Bank to write a poem or short story.

Word Bank					
whack	buzz	hiss	creak	squeal	honk
twang	cuckoo	grind	clink	ping	crack
thump	crash	bow wow	chug	moo	blip
flip flop	squish	beep	smack	chug	chirp
ding dong	rustle	clomp			

_____

_____

_____

_____

_____

_____

_____

_____

_____

_____

_____

_____

Easily Confused Words

Name _____ Date _____

Eating Dessert in the Desert

Word Bank

accept	desert	lose	picture
except	dessert	loose	pitcher
breath	lay	set	
breathe	lie	sit	

Write the word that matches the following definitions. Use the Word Bank if necessary.

1. air that is taken into the lungs and let out _____

2. to recline _____

3. a drawing or a photograph _____

4. to misplace something _____

5. to take what is offered _____

6. a sweet food eaten at the end of a meal _____

7. to put something in a place _____

8. to rest upright in a chair _____

9. not including _____

10. to place _____

11. a container for holding liquid _____

12. to take air in and then let it out _____

13. not firmly attached _____

14. a hot and dry place _____

0-7424-1774-3 *After School Reading Activities*

Name _____ Date _____

About the Book

Write a term for each definition in the blanks.

1. a book's writer ___ ___ ___ ___ ___ R

2. the main idea of a story ___ ___ E ___ ___

3. a person or an animal ___ ___ ___ ___ A ___ ___ ___ ___

4. conversation between characters D ___ ___ ___ ___ ___ ___ ___

5. the turning point ___ ___ ___ ___ A ___

6. the "bad" guy ___ ___ ___ ___ G ___ ___ ___ ___

7. the "good" guy ___ R ___ ___ ___ ___ ___ ___ ___ ___

8. time and place of the action ___ E ___ ___ ___ ___ ___

9. drawings ___ ___ ___ ___ ___ A ___ ___ ___ ___

10. series of events ___ ___ ___ T

B

11. struggle or problem ___ O ___ ___ ___ ___ ___ ___

12. ending ___ ___ ___ ___ ___ ___ ___ ___ O ___

K

Name _____ Date _____

Shortcuts

Match the words in the left column to their abbreviations in the right column.

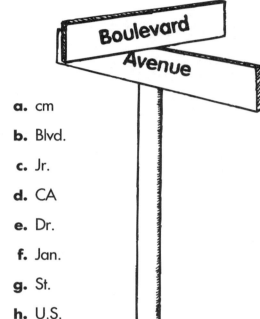

_____ 1. Doctor

_____ 2. Street

_____ 3. Minnesota

_____ 4. Mister

_____ 5. Avenue

_____ 6. centimeter

_____ 7. inch

_____ 8. Boulevard

_____ 9. Junior

_____ 10. Senior

_____ 11. California

_____ 12. January

_____ 13. Monday

_____ 14. United States

_____ 15. dozen

a. cm

b. Blvd.

c. Jr.

d. CA

e. Dr.

f. Jan.

g. St.

h. U.S.

i. Mr.

j. Sr.

k. in.

l. Ave.

m. doz.

n. MN

o. Mon.

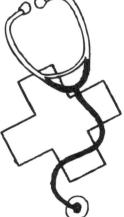

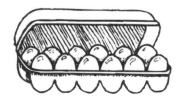

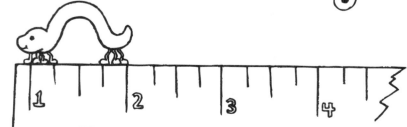

Name _____ Date _____

La Fiesta

Read the following story. Notice the words in italics as you read.

Come for a ride with me just outside of *Santa Fe*. We'll drive through the colorful red rock *canyons* and up onto the *mesa* where the *vista* of the surrounding countryside is spectacular. This is the land of the cowboys. If you look down into the valley, you might see a *rodeo* with cowboys riding bucking *broncos* and throwing their *lassos* to rope a bull's horns. There is a grand house up on the *mesa* that belongs to the Martinez family. Today is the tenth birthday of their daughter Maria, and everyone is invited to her party. The guests gather on the *patio* where tables are laden with *tacos*, *tortilla* chips and *salsa*, *bananas*, *mangos*, and two birthday cakes, one *chocolate* and one *vanilla*. To entertain the guests, a group of musicians are playing *guitars* and *tambourines*.

The best part of the party is the breaking of the *piñata* that hangs from a tree next to the patio. Maria is blindfolded first and handed a stick which she swings at the *piñata* while her papa keeps it moving from side to side and up and down. Smack! Maria hits it. Now it is another child's turn.

After each one tries, the *piñata* finally breaks open. The children rush in as the candy and prizes shower down. They gather as much as they can hold and hurry to give their treasures to their mamas to hold while they rush back for more. As the sun sets over the *mesa*, the air becomes cool, and people put on their *ponchos* for warmth. When the *mosquitoes* come out for their feast, it is time for us to go home.

(continued on page 48)

Name _____ Date _____

La Fiesta (cont.)

The story you just read contains several words in italics that come from the Spanish language. Using the clues below, complete the crossword puzzle with the correct Spanish words from the story.

Across

4. a view
5. a fruit
7. sweet treat made from cocoa
9. event where cowboys display their skills
10. outside porch or paved yard
13. deep cut between mountains
15. an insect
16. sauce made with tomatoes
17. Mexican bread made from corn or wheat flour

Down

1. an untamed horse
2. a rhythm instrument
3. city in New Mexico
4. a flavor
6. a cowboy's rope
8. outer covering, like a blanket with a head hole
11. meat and cheese in a crispy shell
12. decorated papier-maché object filled with candy and treats
14. a string instrument
15. a flat-topped hill

Name _____ Date _____

Sensory Words

The words in the box make you think of seeing, hearing, smelling, or tasting. Write each word in the correct category.

```
┌─────────────────────────────────────────────────┐
│                  Word Bank                        │
│   singing     sweet      piney      dusty         │
│   raindrop    bitter     moldy      barking       │
│   talking     smoky      sour       butterfly     │
│   mooing      books      red        salty         │
└─────────────────────────────────────────────────┘
```

Taste   **Smell**

_____   _____

_____   _____

_____   _____

_____   _____

Hear   **See**

_____   _____

_____   _____

_____   _____

_____   _____

Name _____ Date _____

Code Names

Use the code to write a synonym for each word.

a	c	e	g	h	o	p	r	t	y
1	2	3	4	5	6	7	8	9	10

1. enclose— $\underline{}\ \underline{}\ \underline{}\ \underline{}$
   2 1 4 3

2. inexpensive— $\underline{}\ \underline{}\ \underline{}\ \underline{}\ \underline{}$
   2 5 3 1 7

3. right—
   2 6 8 8 3 2 9

4. transport—
   2 1 8 8 10

5. center—
   2 6 8 3

6. duplicate—
   2 6 7 10

7. pen—
   2 6 6 7

8. table—
   2 5 1 8 9

9. conversation—
   2 5 1 9

10. applaud—
    2 5 3 3 8

11. harvest—
    2 8 6 7

12. crawl—
    2 8 3 3 7

13. concern—
    2 1 8 3

14. capture—
    2 1 9 2 5

15. class—
    2 1 9 3 4 6 8 10

16. price—
    2 5 1 8 4 3

17. stick—
    2 6 5 3 8 3

18. force—
    2 6 3 8 2 3

19. task—
    2 5 6 8 3

20. swindle—
    2 5 3 1 9

Write six words below. Use the code above to write the numbers that spell synonyms to the words. Trade papers with a friend.

21. _____

22. _____

23. _____

24. _____

25. _____

26. _____

Get More from Rumpelstiltskin

Can you find fifty words in the name "Rumpelstiltskin"? List them below.

1. _____
2. _____
3. _____
4. _____
5. _____
6. _____
7. _____
8. _____
9. _____
10. _____
11. _____
12. _____
13. _____
14. _____
15. _____
16. _____
17. _____
18. _____
19. _____
20. _____
21. _____
22. _____
23. _____
24. _____
25. _____
26. _____

27. _____
28. _____
29. _____
30. _____
31. _____
32. _____
33. _____
34. _____
35. _____
36. _____
37. _____
38. _____
39. _____
40. _____
41. _____
42. _____
43. _____
44. _____
45. _____
46. _____
47. _____
48. _____
49. _____
50. _____

Name _____ Date _____

A to Z Names

Can you think of names that begin with each letter of the alphabet?
Write one girl's name and one boy's name for each letter.

A _____   N _____

B _____   O _____

C _____   P _____

D _____   Q _____

E _____   R _____

F _____   S _____

G _____   T _____

H _____   U _____

I _____   V _____

J _____   W _____

K _____   X _____

L _____   Y _____

M _____   Z _____

On another sheet of paper, make a list of animals that begin with each of the letters of the alphabet.

Name _____ Date _____

Compound Fun

Think of a compound word for each of the pictures below. Write it on the line.

1.

_____

5.

_____

2.

_____

6.

_____

3.

_____

7.

_____

4.

_____

8.

_____

On another sheet of paper, draw pictures to represent four more compound words.

Name _____ Date _____

Spell-o-Thon

Practice any vocabulary words using this fun spelling game.

You Need: index cards, marker, box with lid, craft knife, block of foam, ruler, scissors, copy of letters from page 55, copy of directions (below).

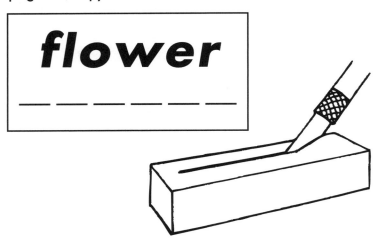

Preparation: Make a copy of the letters on page 55. Laminate, cut apart, and place facedown in the box. Write the vocabulary list of your choice on the index cards, adding lines below the letters equal to the number of letters in each word. Cut the foam into four pieces and slit down the center of each piece about 1/4 inch deep. Make a copy of the directions.

Game is played with two to four players. Place the index cards with the words facedown in the center of the play area. Turn the letters facedown in the box.

Rules for Play: Each player draws five letters from the box and places them in the slit of his piece of foam. The first player turns over the top card so that all players can see it. The object of the game is to spell the word on the card using letters from his set of five. The first player takes any letters from his set that are in the word and puts them in the correct spaces on the card. Then this player draws letters to replace the ones he just laid down. At that same time, this player may also get rid of letters he does not want by putting them upside-down in the lid of the box and replacing them with letters from the box. If the player has none of the letters needed, he does not play. However, this player may turn in one or all of his letters and replace them for the next turn.

At the end of a turn a player will still have five letters in his foam block. The player who completes the word puts the card at the bottom of the stack and places the letters in a separate pile. At the end of the game, the player with the most letters wins. The game continues until there are not enough letters to spell any words.

(continued on page 55)

Spell-o-Thon (cont.)

A	A	A	A	A	A	A	A	A	A	A	A
B	B	B	B	B	C	C	C	C	C	C	D
D	D	D	D	D	D	E	E	E	E	E	E
E	E	E	E	E	E	F	F	F	F	G	G
G	G	G	G	G	G	H	H	H	H	H	H
H	H	I	I	I	I	I	I	I	I	I	I
I	I	J	J	J	K	K	K	K	K	L	L
L	L	L	L	L	L	L	L	M	M	M	M
M	M	M	M	N	N	N	N	N	N	N	N
N	N	O	O	O	O	O	O	O	O	O	O
O	P	P	P	P	P	P	Q	Q	R	R	R
R	R	R	R	R	S	S	S	S	S	S	S
S	S	S	T	T	T	T	T	T	T	T	T
T	T	T	U	U	U	U	U	U	V	V	V
W	W	W	W	W	W	X	Y	Y	Y	Y	Y	Z	Z

The Mystery of a Secret Code

Use the secret code to unlock the mystery words.

A	B	C	D	E	F	G	H	I	J	K	L	M	N	O	P	Q	R	S	T	U	V	W	X	Y	Z
1	2	3	4	5	6	7	8	9	10	11	12	13	14	15	16	17	18	19	20	21	22	23	24	25	26

1. 3–12–21–5–19

_____

2. 19–21–19–16–5–14–19–5

_____

3. 1–12–9–2–9

_____

4. 3–15–14–6–5–19–19–9–15–14

_____

5. 5–22–9–4–5–14–3–5

_____

6. 4–5–4–21–3–20–9–15–14

_____

7. 23–9–20–14–5–19–19

_____

8. 19–21–19–16–5–3–20–19

_____

9. Decode this message.

_____   _____   _____   _____
23-1-20-3-8   15-21-20   6–15–18   20–5–4

_____   _____**!** _____   _____
18-8-5   8-5-18-18-9-14-7-19   20-8-5-25   1–18–5

_____   _____**.**
6–1–12–19–5   3–12–21–5–19

Name _____ Date _____

Compute-a Word

The computer must have a bug in it. It is supposed to use the letters from each word to make three new words. Instead it has done nothing. Help debug it!

Program: Make three new words from each word.

restaurant
1. _____
2. _____
3. _____

understand
1. _____
2. _____
3. _____

dictionary
1. _____
2. _____
3. _____

holiday
1. _____
2. _____
3. _____

milkshake
1. _____
2. _____
3. _____

watermelon
1. _____
2. _____
3. _____

entertainment
1. _____
2. _____
3. _____

Name _____ Date _____

Two Words in One

Write the compound words on the line.

1.

_____

2.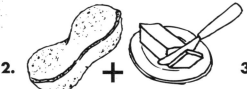

_____

3.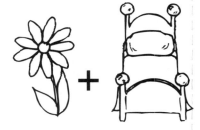

_____

4.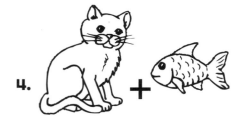

_____

5.

_____

6.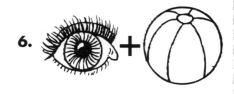

_____

7.

_____

8.

_____

9.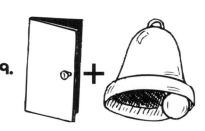

_____

10.  +

_____

11.

_____

12. 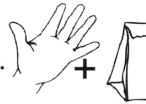 +

_____

Name _____ Date _____

Holiday Happenings

Find the holidays in the wordsearch. Then write the holidays on the lines in the order they occur throughout the year.

St. Patrick's Day   Thanksgiving   Independence Day   April Fool's Day
Columbus Day   Memorial Day   Martin Luther King, Jr. Day Mother's Day
Christmas   Hanukkah   Father's Day   Valentine's Day
Labor Day   New Year's Day Groundhog Day   Halloween

S	M	S	I	Y	A	D	S	R	E	H	T	O	M	T	D	Y	M
V	T	H	A	N	K	S	G	I	V	I	N	G	L	E	A	A	E
A	M	P	H	A	L	L	O	W	E	E	N	R	Y	Y	Y	D	M
L	E	M	A	R	T	I	N	L	K	I	N	G	D	A	Y	E	O
E	M	X	N	T	D	F	B	L	O	I	V	X	B	D	A	C	R
N	O	I	U	E	R	A	U	G	H	N	F	L	Y	G	D	N	I
T	T	I	K	M	S	I	V	X	B	O	R	A	S	O	S	E	A
I	F	M	K	N	E	K	C	P	Q	L	M	B	O	H	R	D	L
N	F	P	A	H	D	R	Y	K	I	D	J	O	T	D	A	N	D
E	B	A	H	I	Q	W	E	E	S	O	P	R	I	N	E	E	A
S	A	M	T	S	I	R	H	C	V	D	N	D	B	U	Y	P	Y
D	F	A	T	H	E	R	S	D	A	Y	A	A	S	O	W	E	B
A	P	R	I	L	F	O	O	L	S	D	A	Y	V	R	E	D	C
Y	L	D	F	T	N	O	R	A	B	D	T	A	S	G	N	N	I
S	T	E	E	W	Y	A	D	S	U	B	M	U	L	O	C	I	K

1. _____
2. _____
3. _____
4. _____
5. _____
6. _____
7. _____
8. _____

9. _____
10. _____
11. _____
12. _____
13. _____
14. _____
15. _____
16. _____

Name _____ Date _____

Palindrome Pals

Mom and Pop are palindromes. Palindromes are words that are spelled the same forward and backward. Use the clues below to discover more palindromes.

1. a young dog   — — —

2. 12:00 P.M.   — — — —

3. horizontally even   — — — — —

4. baby chick sound   — — — —

5. to hang wall covering   — — — — — — —

6. horn sound   — — — —

7. a dipping-into-water-for-apples game   — — —

8. the night before Christmas   — — — —

9. pieces played alone   — — — — —

10. a musical engagement   — — —

11. another name for Pop   — — —

12. radio device to locate objects   — — — — —

13. Indy 500 vehicle (2 words)   — — — — — — —

14. a good work done by a scout   — — — —

15. a female sheep   — — —

16. tiny child   — — —

17. a joke played on someone   — — —

18. opposite of brother   — — —

19. Great! Super!   — — —

20. home of your iris and cornea   — — —

HOW ABOUT TOOT?

Name _____ Date _____

From Whose Point of View?

Read each sentence below. Decide if it is the first or third person's point of view. If it is a first person's point of view, rewrite the sentence to make it a third person's point of view. If it is a third person's point of view, rewrite it to make it a first person's point of view.

1. I wanted to tell Anh and Thant the secret of our leaving, but I had given my word.

_____

2. The grandmother did not want to go aboard the boat.

_____

3. The people on shore were pushing to get on the deck of the boat.

_____

4. Though I had worked for many years in my father's fields, I never considered myself a farmer.

_____

5. Loni made a net from pieces of string and caught a turtle with his new device.

_____

6. I know of a place where we can wash our clothes.

_____

7. The officer looked at them with great interest.

_____

8. When I looked into the harbor, I could see the shapes of whales in the distance.

_____

9. This is my candy, and I choose to share it with everyone on my birthday.

_____

Name _____ Date _____

Bugs Are Good for You

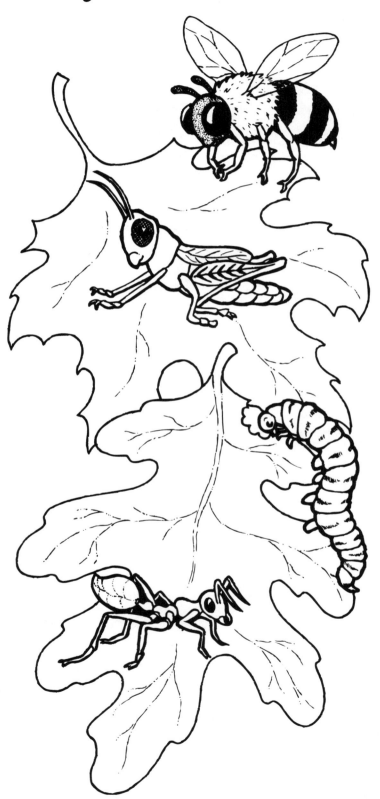

Would you eat bugs? Many people know that bugs taste good and are good for you. In other parts of the world, eating insects is not unusual. Some insects have high nutritional value. Dried insects are 60 to 70 percent protein. Some insects are rich in lycine, an amino acid that helps muscles develop. Other insects are high in iron, zinc, thiamine, or riboflavin. Look at the list of nutrients on the vitamin bottle in your home. You'll see these same items listed. In parts of the world where it is not easy to get vitamin pills, eating insects makes good sense. Some people say that getting nutrients from a food source is a much better way than getting them from a pill.

People eat insects not only because they are healthful, but also because some insects taste great. It is estimated that about 500 different species of insects are eaten somewhere in our world. In Thailand, grasshoppers are a big business. Ant eggs cooked in butter are common in Mexico. Bolivians munch on a type of roasted ant as though they were peanuts. Crickets, caterpillars, termites, bees, and wasps also show up on menus around the world.

Here's some food for thought. It may make you squeamish to think of eating insects, but people from other parts of the world may feel squeamish about eating hen's eggs or escargot—foods that many people around here eat. People learn to like foods that are available to them even if it causes others to feel the way you may right now—YUCK.

(continued on page 63)

Name _____ Date _____

Bugs Are Good for You (cont.)

Place a check mark on the line in front of the best answer to each question.

1. What is the main idea of the entire reading selection?

_____ Vitamin pills are good for you.

_____ Some people eat insects for nutritional value and taste.

_____ You have to go to a fancy restaurant to eat escargot.

2. Read the first paragraph of the passage again. What is the main idea?

_____ Everyone needs iron in his or her diet.

_____ It is necessary to take vitamin pills to stay healthy.

_____ Some insects have high nutritional value.

3. Read the second paragraph of the passage. What is the main idea?

_____ People in Bolivia don't like peanuts.

_____ Some people eat insects because they taste great.

_____ You can eat insects.

4. Read the final paragraph. What is the author's main point?

_____ Food can help you think.

_____ The French eat snails, too.

_____ People from other parts of the world may think we eat strange things.

People have different tastes. List four unusual foods that you like that your friends may not like. Star the food that is also healthy.

_____

_____

_____

_____

Name _____ Date _____

Deep in the Earth

Earth is covered with rocks of various sizes, colors, and shapes. Rocks may be formed in different ways. Three kinds of rocks are igneous rocks, sedimentary rocks, and metamorphic rocks.

Igneous rocks are formed from extremely high temperatures. Deep inside the earth's core is hot, liquid rock called magma. Magma may be forced through cracks in the earth. As it moves away from the hot core, it cools and forms igneous rock. Sometimes liquid rock is forced to the surface of the earth through volcanoes. When lava from a volcano cools, it forms igneous rock.

Sedimentary rock is formed when loose materials are pressed together over time. These loose materials may be small stones, sand, and decomposed plants and animals. Often the materials accumulate on the

bottom of the ocean. The water may dissolve or get pressed out. The loose materials get cemented together as they harden into rock.

Metamorphic rocks are rocks that have been formed by some major change. Pressure and heat can change igneous and sedimentary rocks into metamorphic rocks. Through heat and pressure, the metamorphic rock may change the way it looks or even its mineral makeup.

Each of these rocks can be found on the earth's crust. You can study a rock's properties to help identify whether it is igneous, sedimentary, or metamorphic.

(continued on page 65)

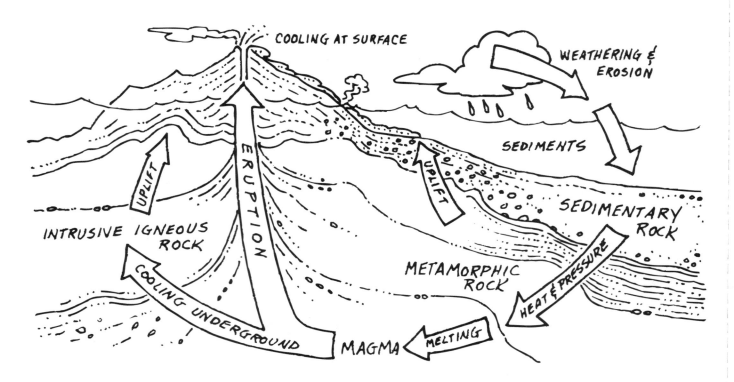

Deep in the Earth (cont.)

Refer to the article to complete the following.

1. Use one word to name the topic of this passage. _____

2. The main idea of the passage is . . .
_____ Fossils are trapped in rocks.
_____ Igneous rocks are formed from magma.
_____ Rocks are formed three ways.

3. Fill in the web. Write the topic sentence in the first oval. Write the three sub-topics in the next three ovals. Fill in the rest of the ovals with the supporting details.

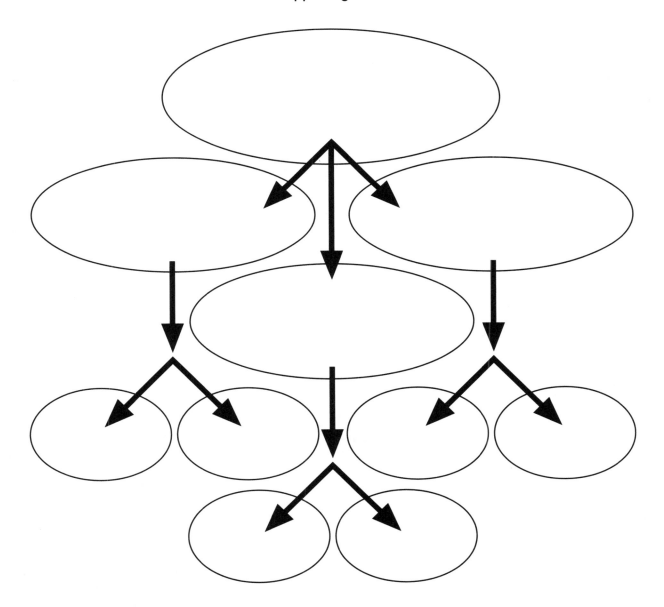

Name _____ Date _____

X Marks the Spot

	A	B	C	D	E	F	G
7							
6							
5							
4							
3							
2							
1							

1. In B5, draw a big **X**.
2. In E7, draw a smiling face.
3. Color box G1 red.
4. Write your first name in box D4.
5. In A1, draw a star and color it yellow.
6. Color all of row 2 green.
7. Draw a purple heart in F3.
8. In A7, draw a flower with pink petals.
9. Write your favorite number in box E5.
10. Draw a dollar sign in G6.
11. Draw a tree in A4.
12. Write your birthday in box D1.

Name _____ Date _____

Down the Drain

Let's look at how we use water and how we can save water.

1. Write the names of three oceans in the upper right corner of this page.

2. The average American uses 60 gallons of water a day. Draw a large glass of water to the left of the shower. Estimate the number of gallons an American would use in a year and write it on the glass.

3. The average bath uses 50 gallons of water. A five-minute shower uses 25 gallons, or half the water of a bath. Write the fraction one-half on the shower curtain.

4. A special "low flow" shower head adds air to the water and cuts the water used by half again. Write the two rhyming words used here above the shower.

5. Describe what a day without water would be like on the back of this paper.

6. Running the rinse water while washing dishes wastes 30 gallons. In the upper left corner, write four verbs that tell what to do when washing dishes.

7. Running the water while you brush your teeth wastes about five gallons of water. Draw five 1-gallon milk jugs in the lower right corner. Figure out how many quarts of water this would be. Write your problem on the milk jugs.

8. It takes five to seven gallons of water to flush a toilet. Multiply the number of people in your house by five and write that number to the right of the shower curtain.

9. On the back of this paper, write one way you will try to save water.

10. To get a better idea of just how much 60 gallons is, collect 60 empty one-gallon milk jugs as a class project. Then be sure to recycle them.

Name _____ Date _____

Find the Effect

Read the causes below. Choose the correct effect for each of the pictures and write the letter on the line.

_____ **1.** Maria ran a long race.

_____ **2.** The drought lasted a month.

_____ **3.** The electricity went out last night.

_____ **4.** A tornado zoomed toward her house.

_____ **5.** Flames rose from the abandoned building.

_____ **6.** Ocean waves pounded the shore.

a. She couldn't water her yard.

e. She was tired.

b. The sandcastle washed away.

c. Fire trucks zipped down the street.

f. She couldn't see a thing.

d. She ran to the basement for shelter.

If—Then

Match the sentence parts that go together best. Write the number of the first sentence on the line in front of the last part for each one.

1. If you baby-sit for me Saturday night,

2. If you are nice,

3. If we leave work by 4:30,

4. If you leave a note on your door,

5. If you don't have enough money for the movie,

6. If my father isn't too tired,

7. If the wind keeps up,

8. If you want to get a seat at the concert,

9. If our neighbor cuts the grass early Sunday morning,

10. If the plant doesn't feel damp,

11. If my house were painted white,

12. If everyone talked at the same time,

13. If you don't get a haircut,

14. If the teakettle whistles,

15. If no one answers the door,

16. If the little boy crosses the street,

17. If the horse is tired,

18. If you have a long fork,

19. If you don't want any dessert,

20. If a king comes into the room,

21. If it snows a lot tomorrow,

_____ **a.** the delivery man will leave the package.

_____ **b.** it needs to be watered.

_____ **c.** you could roast marshmallows.

_____ **d.** probably no one is at home.

_____ **e.** everyone will rise.

_____ **f.** I'll pay you double.

_____ **g.** the water is boiling.

_____ **h.** tomorrow will be a great kite-flying day.

_____ **i.** let him rest.

_____ **j.** no one could hear directions.

_____ **k.** we will avoid rush hour.

_____ **l.** say, "No thank you."

_____ **m.** the noise will wake me up.

_____ **n.** we can build an igloo.

_____ **o.** he said he would show me how to shoot baskets.

_____ **p.** it would look like a miniature White House.

_____ **q.** I'll loan you the rest.

_____ **r.** he must hold on to his mother's hand.

_____ **s.** you will have many friends.

_____ **t.** you will have to be at the auditorium early.

_____ **u.** you will have long hair.

Name _____ Date _____

The Greatest Gift

Read the story. Then answer the questions on page 71.

Rena dabbed her paintbrush across her palette. She brushed the color across the canvas. *I'll never be able to do it*, she thought. She gazed at the painting on the wall of the art studio.

"Rena," said her art teacher. "What you've done here is beautiful! You have such talent. You're one of my best students because you have such an unusual style."

Rena shook her head. "Maybe, but my work will never look like that." She looked again at the painting hanging on the wall.

When Rena walked in the door at home, her little brother grabbed her by the arm. "Rena, Rena, will you make a picture for Grandpa's birthday? I wrote a poem for him, but I want to put it with a great big picture. And I want you to do it because you're such a great artist."

Rena smiled. "Okay, Oscar. Grab all those old pictures from the box."

Oscar skipped out of the room. A few minutes later, he dashed in, carrying Grandpa's photos. It was hard to piece them together because they were all torn, and they were faded, too.

At the art studio, Rena laid the torn and faded photos across a table so she could arrange them in a special way. For weeks, Rena worked with her paints on a big canvas. She placed every stroke and chose every color with great care.

On Grandpa's birthday, Oscar read his poem. Then Rena gave Grandpa the painting. Tears filled Grandpa's eyes. "The poem was wonderful, and the painting . . . the painting shows my old friends and my old neighborhood in a way that makes me feel as though I'm there all over again. Rena, you've shown me how special all these people have been in my life. You and Oscar are wonderful."

(continued on page 71)

Name _____ Date _____

The Greatest Gift (cont.)

Answer these cause and effect questions about the story on page 70. Use complete sentences.

1. Why did Rena's art teacher like Rena's work?

_____

_____

_____

_____

2. Why did Oscar want Rena to paint a picture for Grandpa?

_____

_____

_____

_____

3. Why was it hard to piece together Grandpa's old photos?

_____

_____

_____

_____

4. Why did Grandpa cry when he saw Rena's painting?

_____

_____

_____

_____

Name _____ Date _____

Make It

Write 1–4 to put the sentences in order. Then draw the correct picture in the cloud.

○ Pour the mixture into the muffin tins.

○ Serve the hot blueberry muffins with butter.

○ Place the muffin tins in the oven.

○ Mix flour, eggs, milk, and blueberries.

Draw: Sentence 4

○ Write a message on the valentine.

○ Cut hearts from red and white paper.

○ Give the valentine to a friend.

○ Paste the hearts to make a valentine.

Draw: Sentence 3

○ Serve the milkshake with a spoon and a straw.

○ Turn the blender on and mix for two minutes.

○ Pour milk, sugar, and ice cream into a blender.

○ Pour the yummy milkshake into a glass.

Draw: Sentence 1

○ Cut ten squares of yellow paper.

○ Mail the party invitations to friends.

○ Write a party invitation on each square.

○ Put each invitation in an envelope.

Draw: Sentence 2

Name _____ Date _____

Putting It All Together

Juanita bought a dinosaur-shaped table as a birthday present for her little brother. The entire table came in a box that was almost flat. Before she started to put the table together, Juanita took out the pieces and read the directions. You can see the directions here.

1. Check to be sure you have all the pieces: one tabletop, four table legs, eight small screws, and four large screws.

2. Snap the table legs into the tabletop holes.

3. Screw in the large screws under the tabletop to hold the legs tight.

4. Screw the small screws into the tabletop where marked.

Answer these questions using the directions above.

1. Suppose that Juanita has already opened the box and checked the pieces. What should she do second? How do you know?

_____

2. Should she screw the large screws under the tabletop before or after she screws in the small ones? How do you know?

_____

3. Why is it important for Juanita to be certain that she has all the pieces before she begins to put the table together? What might she do with the screws to be certain that she doesn't lose them?

_____

_____

4. On a separate sheet of paper, use what you know to write a paragraph explaining how to put the table together. Use a topic sentence and words such as first, second, next, and last as you write your paragraph.

Name _____ Date _____

Right Back at You

Perhaps you have heard that many types of bats have very small eyes and do not see well. Still, as they swoop through the night, they do not bump into objects and are able to find food, even though they cannot see their prey. How is this possible? Echolocation!

You might recognize the beginning of the word echolocation as *echo*, and you might recognize the last part of the word as *location*. This gives you clues about how echolocation works. The bat sends out sounds. The sounds bounce off objects and return to the bat. Echolocation not only tells the bat that objects are nearby. It also tells the bat just how far away the objects are.

Bats are not the only creatures who use echolocation. Porpoises and some types of whales and birds use it as well.

Answer the questions about the passage you have just read.

1. Why did the author most likely write this passage?
Circle one reason below and tell why you made your choice.

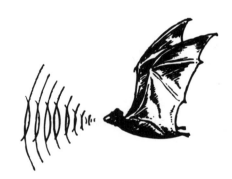

- to convince you to visit bats

- to tell you a funny story about bats

- to give you information about bats

- to describe feelings about bats

_____

_____

2. On a separate sheet of paper, write a passage about dogs using facts you know.
Write your passage for the same reason the author of "Right Back at You" wrote about bats.

Name _____ Date _____

The Soldier's Lucky Coin

Read this story and use it to answer the questions on page 76.

George Dixon prepared to leave to fight in the United States Civil War. He was engaged to be married, and the woman he was engaged to gave him something special, a gold twenty-dollar coin, as a good-luck token.

Dixon fought for his cause. During one battle, a bullet zipped toward his leg. Unbelievably, he was not harmed. Instead of hitting his leg, the bullet hit the gold coin he always carried in his pocket. The bullet bent the coin, but Dixon's leg was fine. The special gift from his sweetheart had kept him safe. Because of this, he had a special message written on the coin. The message listed the name of the battle and the date when the coin had saved his life.

Dixon left the battlefield to take command of a submarine. Dixon's submarine mysteriously sank and he was never seen again. What happened to Dixon? And what happened to the gold coin?

People heard about Dixon's story after the Civil War. Many believed that it was just a sweet story, a fable, or a bit of fiction. Others believed that it might be true.

Scientists have now found the remains of the H. L. Hunley, Dixon's submarine. When they first saw the submarine, it lay across the ocean floor. Archaeologists and other scientists searched through the submarine to learn more about it. They decided to bring the submarine up from the ocean floor so that others could see it.

One scientist reached down into a muddy area as preparations were made to show the submarine to the public. She felt ridges, the lines around the edge of a coin. A great thrill came over her. Carefully, she pulled out the coin. It was a very exciting moment when she realized what she was holding in her hand. It was a bent twenty-dollar coin with the same special message etched into it.

(continued on page 76)

Name _____ Date _____

The Soldier's Lucky Coin (cont.)

Use the story on page 75 to answer the questions below.

1. Was the story of the lucky soldier fact or fiction? How do you know?

_____

_____

2. Was the coin the scientist found the same coin George Dixon had lost? How do you know?

_____

_____

3. What is the main reason the author wrote this passage? Circle one of the answer choices.

    a. to describe feelings about lost coins

    b. to give you information about a lost coin

    c. to convince you to study lost coins

    d. to create a fun fiction passage

4. Explain why you chose the answer to number three.

_____

_____

5. Write a paragraph describing a time you found a lost item. Include a description of the item and the way you went about finding it.

_____

_____

_____

_____

_____

_____

_____

Name _____ Date _____

An "Egg"citing Discovery

I discovered a gray egg in my yard.
Its shell is large and very hard.
I know it must be very old,
'Cuz it's surrounded by a lot of mold.

When my reptile hatches, I'll be so proud!
Its baby cry will be so loud.
We'll go walking, it will look distinct,
Towering above me—it's NOT extinct!

1. What kind of animal does the speaker think will hatch out of the egg?

_____

2. Name three clues that helped you guess its identity.

   a. _____

   b. _____

   c. _____

3. If you found this egg, would you think it would hatch or not? _____

   Why or why not? _____

_____

Name _____ Date _____

Big Dreams

When I grow up, I am going to build a huge store where boys and girls can find any toy imaginable. There will be one room filled with life-size dolls that can walk, run, skate, talk, eat, smile, and even read a book with you.

Another room will be filled with cars and trucks that kids can actually drive (after fastening their seatbelts, of course).

Game boards will be so huge that the kids can become living pieces that move. How many games do you play now where the pieces walk to the next square?

One room will be devoted to computers. Each kid will move the mouse so that the characters will seem to jump off the screen.

If anyone is interested in puzzles, he or she can play in my puzzle room. Life-size, three-dimensional puzzles can be put together, pulled apart, and put together again.

Another room will be the size of a football field. Here kids will be able to bounce, throw, and hit balls without having to hear their parents say to them, "You have to play outside with those balls!"

(continued on page 79)

Name _____ Date _____

Big Dreams (cont.)

The best part of my store would be that it never closes. Kids could stay as long as they wanted! Also, they would not have to pay for anything!

Parents, or any other adults, would not be allowed in my store! I would make the door so tiny that only kids would be able to enter.

I guess I have thought of everything, except . . . Oops! There could be one, big problem . . .

1. What is the real problem that the speaker is thinking about at the end of the story?

_____

_____

2. How can you tell that the speaker is "safety-conscious"?

_____

_____

3. Circle the words that describe how the speaker feels as he tells of his big plans.

content   indifferent   motivated   tranquil   enthusiastic   excited

4. Is the speaker very realistic? _____ Why or why not? _____

_____

_____

5. Circle all true statements.

The toy store will be the same size as a football field.

The toy store will be larger than a football field.

The speaker hates all adults.

Children would probably enjoy playing in his store.

6. Would you like to visit this toy store? _____ Explain. _____

_____

_____

Name _____ Date _____

How a Mosquito Bites

Does anyone like mosquitoes? Although the mosquito's high-pitched hum may be attractive to male mosquitoes, it signals danger to humans. When a mosquito "bites," it hurts, next it itches, and then we need to scratch.

We talk about mosquito "bites," but actually mosquitoes don't bite. They stab and sip their victim's blood. Only the female mosquito "bites" us since she needs blood for the development of the eggs inside her body.

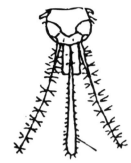

Look at the illustration that shows the front view of the female mosquito.

Notice the long tube-like proboscis. This is the mosquito's mouth. The proboscis stabs its victim, and then acts like a straw to sip the blood. A female mosquito may drink the blood of humans, frogs, birds, or other animals. A male will sip from plants. Liquids are the mosquito's only diet.

The next illustrations show the side view of the mosquito's head and how the mosquito "bites."

Locate the stylets. When the mosquito "bites," it stabs through the victim's skin with six needle-like stylets, which form the center of the proboscis. Notice how the stylets poke into the skin, and then bend to enter a blood vessel. While the mosquito is sucking the blood, it leaves saliva under the person's skin. Most of us are allergic to this saliva. That's what makes us itch.

Mosquitoes also spread harmful diseases. Certain mosquitoes carry the germs that cause diseases such as malaria and yellow fever. They leave germs when they "bite." Many of the mosquitoes that spread diseases live in hot, moist lands near the equator. But the mosquitoes are found in all parts of the world—even the Arctic.

(continued on page 81)

0-7424-1774-3 *After School Reading Activities*

Name _____ Date _____

How a Mosquito Bites (cont.)

Using the information from the passage on page 80, answer these questions.

1. What diseases can some mosquitoes spread?

_____

_____

2. In what climate do the mosquitoes that spread diseases live?

_____

_____

3. Why is it inaccurate to say that a mosquito bites?

_____

_____

4. How is a mosquito's mouth like a straw?

_____

_____

5. After a mosquito "bites" us, what makes us itch?

_____

_____

6. Why does only the female mosquito need to suck blood?

_____

_____

7. Put a check in front of the statements that are correct.

_____ Both male and female suck blood.

_____ A male mosquito does not have a proboscis.

_____ A mosquito can open its jaws wide to take a big bite.

_____ Mosquitoes eat plant juice.

My First Job, Part One

Mrs. Bradford smiled broadly as she let me in the house. "Cassie, you don't realize how grateful Mr. Bradford and I are to see you! We were afraid we wouldn't be able to get a babysitter on such short notice. We will be home about midnight. Here's a list of instructions and an emergency number to call if necessary."

"Bye, Bart!" Mr. and Mrs. Bradford both said. "Be sure to listen to Cassie!" They kissed him on the cheek and left.

After they left, I read Mrs. Bradford's note. It said:

Cassie,

1. **Warm spaghetti in the microwave and feed Bart.**

2. **Give Bart a bath and put on his pajamas.**

3. **Play a game with Bart.**

4. **Put Bart to bed.**

5. **Relax and watch television until we return.**

In case of emergency,

please call 838–3083.

"Simple enough," I thought as I put the note down and headed for the kitchen to feed Bart.

I found the spaghetti in the refrigerator. As I placed the container in the microwave, little Bart stood in front of the open refrigerator and put his hands in a bowl of chocolate pudding.

"No, Bart!" I said firmly as I pulled him away.

"Cassie want some?" Bart asked as he laid his hands on my mouth and all across my face.

I quickly wiped his hands and my face and lowered him into his chair. After heating the spaghetti, I began to feed him dinner.

"No spaghetti!" Bart screeched defiantly. "Gimme a hot dog!"

"Sorry, Bart," I apologized, "but . . ." Before I

(continued on page 83)

My First Job, Part One (cont.)

could finish, Bart threw the bowl of spaghetti at my head and jumped down onto the floor.

"Bart! Come back!" I yelled as I chased him into the living room, leaving a trail of spaghetti as I went. I finally caught him at the piano rubbing his hands across the keys, and I carried him back to the kitchen and made him eat the little bit of spaghetti that remained in the bowl. Then I checked the first item off Mrs. Bradford's list.

Next on the list was Bart's bath. He certainly needed one. This time I wasn't going to let him out of my sight.

1. Briefly describe Cassie. _____

_____

_____

_____

_____

2. Briefly describe Bart. _____

_____

_____

_____

3. Write a brief summary of the three ways in which Bart created mischief for Cassie.

   a. _____

   b. _____

   c. _____

My First Job, Part Two

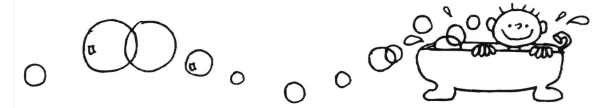

I carried Bart while I got a towel and his pajamas. I even held him while I ran the bath water, making sure that the temperature was perfect. I poured a small amount of bubble bath into the tub. As I lowered Bart slowly into the water, he grabbed the bubble bath and dumped the whole thing into the tub!

"Oh, well," I thought. "At least he'll get really clean."

Soon, bubbles were everywhere! Bart splashed and splashed until every surface was wet. Finally, I rinsed Bart off, dried him, and with some effort, put on his pajamas. I checked off the second item on my list.

"Hmmm," I muttered as I checked the list again. "What kind of game should we play?"

"Cassie build a house!" Bart shouted as I dodged flying building blocks.

"Okay, Bart," I agreed, "but you have to sit perfectly still!" I was surprised that he listened as I built four walls around him.

"This was pretty easy," I thought.

But I had spoken too soon. Bart suddenly stood up and kicked his legs at the blocks, sending them all flying around the room.

I groaned as I checked item number three from my list and said, "It's time for bed."

That announcement triggered a running marathon all through the house until I cornered Bart in the living room closet. I carried him up to his bedroom, and amazingly, he fell asleep almost immediately.

I cleaned and cleaned until the house was immaculate. I turned on the television, plopped exhausted on the couch, and heard the door slowly open.

"Cassie, we're back," said Mr. Bradford in a hushed voice.

"The house looks great!" said Mrs. Bradford. "By the way, we would like to know if you can come back again tomorrow."

"Uh . . . I don't think so, Mrs. Bradford. I'm pretty busy until next year—I mean next week."

While I lay in bed that night, I kept thinking that maybe someone had reversed a couple of letters in Bart's name.

(continued of page 85)

My First Job, Part Two (cont.)

1. Briefly describe two times that Bart created mischief for Cassie.

a. _____

_____

b. _____

_____

2. Here is Mrs. Bradford's list of jobs for Cassie. Number the jobs in the order of their occurrence.

_____ **Put Bart to bed.**

_____ **Give Bart a bath.**

_____ **Warm spaghetti and feed Bart.**

_____ **Relax. Watch television until we return.**

_____ **Play a game or play with toys.**

Name _____ Date _____

Jumping to Conclusions

Write your own conclusion to each of the following situations.

1. Your brother just turned five. He has chocolate all over his face and he looks sheepish.

_____
_____
_____

2. Your parents are gone. It's 9:00 P.M. and you hear a thump and a cry.

_____
_____
_____

3. You are making a cake. You hear the sound of beating wings and a thin, shrill squeal.

_____
_____
_____

4. You are outdoors after dark during summer vacation. You see a sudden flash of light and smell a smoky odor.

_____
_____
_____

5. One morning at school you see your friend looking dreamy-eyed. On her paper she has drawn hearts and flowers.

_____
_____
_____

6. A large column of clouds appears in the western sky, and a strong wind starts blowing.

_____
_____
_____

Now describe a new situation on the back of this paper. Include four important details and make up a conclusion in your head. Have a friend read your situation and try to guess your conclusion.

Context Clues

Name _____ Date _____

Scrambled Words

Unscramble the letters in parentheses to spell a word that makes sense in each sentence.

1. Cookies don't _____ to me; I prefer candy.
(papale)

2. The desert is a good place to see a _____.
(saccut)

3. When is Halley's _____ supposed to appear again?
(tomec)

4. Take a deep breath and then _____.
(elahex)

5. Place the _____ in the can before pouring the gasoline.
(nenulf)

6. I am learning how to do _____ tricks.
(gicam)

7. "I don't have a _____ thing to wear!" complained Jill.
(gilens)

8. An _____ is made of sun-dried bricks.
(bedoa)

9. Is _____ ice cream your favorite?
(alaviln)

10. This word scramble is _____ too difficult for me.
(splimy)

11. Mother set the china on the _____ tablecloth.
(ennil)

12. I am _____ for chocolate chip cookies.
(gurhyn)

13. I wish you much _____ on your new job.
(usseccs)

14. How many people are employed at that _____?
(tarfocy)

15. Hold your breath to help get rid of the _____.
(spuchic)

 0-7424-1774-3 *After School Reading Activities*

Name _____ Date _____

Look for the Clues

Circle the word or phrase that is closest in meaning to the underlined word.

1. The students enjoyed a <u>reprieve</u> from their work while playing outside.

        grade   rest   headache

2. Aunt Betty <u>lavishes</u> gifts on us each time we visit her in Minnesota.

        places upon   greatly enjoys   generously gives

3. Father felt <u>exasperated</u> when he couldn't get the van running.

        happy   annoyed   hopeful

4. Mark placed his folded jeans in the old <u>chiffonier</u> in his bedroom.

        toy box   bookcase   dresser

5. Summer is the <u>optimal</u> time for swimming and playing at the beach.

        best   weather   last

6. Marta <u>reciprocated</u> John's kindness by bringing him a gift.

        enjoyed   noticed   returned

7. It is <u>essential</u> to wear a warm coat and hat on a cold wintry day.

        necessary   good   easy

8. Everyone seems to like Dan because he is always <u>amiable</u>.

        angry   friendly   sad

0-7424-1774-3 *After School Reading Activities*

Name _____ Date _____

A Class of Its Own

Read the words in each list. Cross out the word in each that does not belong with the other words. Write the name of the category on the line.

1. _____**Birds**_____

duck

pelican

~~snake~~

turkey

parrot

2. _____

math

movie

science

spelling

history

3. _____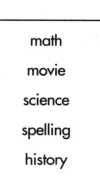

apple

corn

pear

watermelon

peach

4. _____

boxer

poodle

dachshund

collie

lion

5. _____

tulip

rose

violet

pink

daisy

6. _____

Maryland

Florida

Chicago

California

Indiana

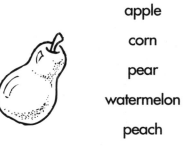

Write your own words to go in each category below.

Languages	Hobbies	Colors
1. _____	1. _____	1. _____
2. _____	2. _____	2. _____
3. _____	3. _____	3. _____
4. _____	4. _____	4. _____
5. _____	5. _____	5. _____
6. _____	6. _____	6. _____

Name _____ Date _____

Similes Are Like . . .

Similes are phrases that describe nouns or verbs by comparing them with other objects. They always use the words "as" or "like." Read the examples:

The baby was as cute as a button.

The rock is like rough sandpaper.

Complete the following similes by matching the first part of the sentence to a phrase that makes sense. Draw a line from column one to its match in column two.

Column One	**Column Two**
1. The eggshell was as white as	a star.
2. The mountain was as high as	a rock.
3. The diamond sparkled like	an ox.
4. The angry dog growled like	the moon.
5. The man was as strong as	a deer.
6. The stale bread was as hard as	a bear.
7. The turtle was as slow as	molasses.
8. The athlete ran like	snow.

Now use the Word Bank to fill in both parts of the following similes.

Word Bank					
clown	clay	ice	hyena	dough	popsicle

1. The _____ was as cold as _____ .

2. The _____ felt like _____ .

3. The _____ laughed like a _____ .

Name _____ Date _____

Is That True?

Fiction is writing that doesn't always use real or true characters and events. In nonfiction, the writer sets down facts about our world and real events as they happened.

Read each pair of statements below. If the statement is an example of nonfiction, write **NF** on the line next to it. Put an **F** next to each statement that is an example of fiction.

1. _____ Turtles have hard shells.

   _____ Turtles use their hard shells to play hide and seek.

2. _____ The elf made a dress out of leaves.

   _____ Leaves come in many shapes, sizes, and colors.

3. _____ The thermometer showed the temperature was below freezing.

   _____ The thermometer put on a coat to keep warm in the freezing cold.

4. _____ Ladybugs have wings.

   _____ Ladybugs are grouchy.

5. _____ Cows can jump over the moon.

   _____ Milk comes from cows.

6. _____ Baseball is played with a bat and a ball.

   _____ The bat told the baseball, "You're going for a ride!"

7. _____ The mice in the attic sewed a ball dress.

   _____ Mice live in the attics of some older homes.

Now write two sentences on the back of this paper and have a friend tell you if it is fiction or nonfiction.

0-7424-1774-3 *After School Reading Activities*

Name _____ Date _____

Football and Soccer

Read the following information about football and soccer. Then fill in the Venn diagram to show the similarities and differences between the two sports.

Football is played mainly in the United States and Canada. It is played with an oval ball on a field that is about 110 meters long and 49 meters wide.* It is played with two teams of 11 players each. The players are required to wear protective equipment because of the game's physical contact, which includes tackling. The game starts with a kickoff. Then players run or pass the ball to try to score a touchdown, which is six points.

Soccer is played all over the world. It is played with a round ball on a field that varies from 91–119 meters long and 46–91 meters wide. It is played with two teams of 11 players each. Shin guards are the only protective gear worn. The game starts with a kickoff. Then players kick or head the ball to try to score a goal, which is one point.

(*In yards: 120 x 53.33)

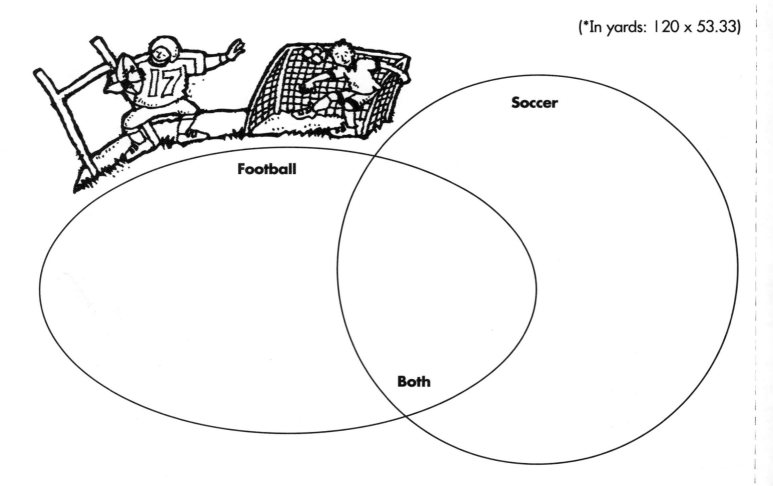

Football   Soccer

Both

Name _____ Date _____

The White House Gang

The White House is the large house in which our president lives. Can you imagine living there? The six children of one president thought it was great fun. Theodore Roosevelt, our twenty-sixth president, moved into the White House with his wife, four boys, and two girls. The Roosevelt children loved playing with each other and their father. Some people called these children "the White House gang" because of the mischief they got into so often.

The Roosevelt children had many pets, including an enormous blue parrot named Eli. They also kept a bear, a lizard, a one-legged rooster, a barn owl, a rabbit, a pig, and a pony. One time, one of Roosevelt's sons rode the pony upstairs to see his sick brother. Another time, the children spit paper balls at a picture of President Andrew Jackson. They also sent their father a note saying they had gone to war with the White House. In fun, their father asked for peace through his war department. The Roosevelt children got into much mischief while they lived at the White House.

1. Put a check in front of the main idea of the story.

_____ The president's children had many unusual pets.

_____ President Roosevelt loved his mischief-making children.

_____ One of Roosevelt's sons rode a pony upstairs.

_____ Most presidents have children.

_____ The Roosevelt children had fun while living in the White House.

_____ Everyone wants to live in the White House.

2. Circle the correct sentence.

The White House gang got into mischief in the White House.

The White House gang robbed banks and were sent to jail.

(continued on page 94)

The White House Gang (cont.)

3. In your own words, write what *mischief* means. _____

_____

4. Tell about some mischievous things the Roosevelt children did in the White House.

_____

_____

_____

5. In complete sentences, explain what you think about the mischief the children created.

_____

_____

6. Make an outline of the story on a separate sheet of paper. Be sure to include the main idea.

7. What kinds of pets did the gang have? _____

_____

8. Which of these pets would you want? Explain why. _____

_____

9. What did President Roosevelt do when his children sent him a note saying they had declared war with the White House? _____

_____

10. Write the names of three other United States presidents. _____

_____

11. On the back of this paper, draw a picture of you and a pet standing next to the White House.

12. On page 93, color the horse brown, the pig pink, the parrot blue, and the rooster red.

Name _____ Date _____

A Big, Hairy Spider

A tarantula is a big, hairy spider. You might have seen one in a pet shop that carries spiders and other unusual pets. In our country, tarantulas live in the west, where it is hot and dry. During the day, tarantulas sleep in holes and other dark places. They come out at night to hunt for food.

Tarantulas catch their food mostly by jumping on it and biting it. Smaller tarantulas eat insects. Larger ones eat mice and lizards. A tarantula's poison can kill the animals it hunts, but its poison cannot kill a human. If you are bitten, you will soon know that a tarantula bite hurts only about as much as a bee sting. Its bite helps this spider protect itself. Tarantulas are shy spiders. They bite humans only if they feel threatened and cannot get away.

A tarantula has another way to protect itself. It can rub its hind legs together, which causes its stiff leg hairs to fly up in the air. Each tiny hair can make a hurtful skin or eye wound.

The tarantula got its name from a big wolf spider that lives near Taranto, Italy. This wolf spider looks similar to tarantulas. People in Taranto used to think that anyone bitten by the wolf spider would get a disease called *tarantism*. They claimed that a person with that disease would jump in the air and make loud sounds. Today, we know this story is untrue. We also know that tarantulas are not the same as wolf spiders.

Circle the best answer based on information you learned from the story.

1. If you visit a pet shop that carries unusual pets, you might see a

   cat.   puppy.   tarantula.   canary.

2. Poking or touching a tarantula might make it

   run away.   bite you.   run after you until it catches you.

3. Someone who has been bitten by a tarantula will

   jump in the air, dance, and scream.   feel a bite like a bee sting.

(continued on page 96)

Mixed Skills

A Big, Hairy Spider (cont.)

Fill in the blanks with what you think would happen, based on information in the story.

4. If a lizard stopped near a dark hole at night in the desert, what might happen? _____

_____

5. Explain two things that might happen if a person picked up a tarantula.

a. _____

b. _____

6. What might you see if you were to carefully check a hole or other dark place in a desert?

_____

7. Someone who reaches carelessly into a hole or under a rock might _____

_____.

8. If you took a tarantula home, what might happen? _____

_____

9. Like you, tarantulas need food each day, and they eat only certain things. If you could not find the right food for a pet tarantula, what would probably happen?

_____

10. If you got down on your knees to look closely at a tarantula that was rubbing its hind legs together, what might happen? _____

_____

_____

11. Where did the tarantula get its name? _____

12. Write a definition for *tarantism*. _____

_____

Name _____ Date _____

Two Friends, Two Problems

Read the two letters. Then fill in the chart to contrast the two characters' problems.

Dear Dennis,

Well, here I am at my aunt's house. How am I ever going to get everything she wants done? I only got to sit down for five minutes before she had me painting the stairs. She wants to wash the walls in the kitchen. She wants me to wax the floor in the hallway. And did I tell you about the barn? She wants me to clean out all the old hay in the barn! It's got to be hundred-year-old hay! Every night I fall into bed, and then it feels like I get two minutes of sleep before it is morning again. I sure hope I survive and see you at school in September!

Ralph

Dear Dennis,

Hey, I miss you! It is so quiet here at my grandmother's house. She doesn't own a TV! She must be the last person on the planet without one. All morning long, we sit and read, then we eat lunch, then we go for a little walk. After that, we read some more. The only time I get to see anyone is when we shop for groceries. Plus, Grandma won't let me help her with anything. If I offer to wash the dishes, she says, "No, dear, you are on vacation." If I offer to weed the garden, she says, "Oh, no, dear, I always do that." She even makes my bed! I hope I don't die of boredom before school starts!

Sheila

	Ralph	**Sheila**
1. Where is each friend staying?	_____	_____
2. What is each friend's problem?	_____	_____
3. Describe in one word how each friend feels.	_____	_____
4. What is the solution for each friend's problem?	_____	_____

0-7424-1774-3 *After School Reading Activities*

Name _____ Date _____

Details, Details

Not every sentence in a story contains an important event. Details help you imagine what is going on as you read. Read the story. Then answer the questions on page 99.

Billy knew that he was in trouble... big trouble. Ms. Keaton, his teacher, had seen him cheating on his test. She hadn't said anything yet, but Billy knew that she'd seen him peek at the little piece of paper hidden in his hand. He chewed on his pencil for a minute and thought. He had to get rid of that paper. But how?

"Billy, if you are finished with your test, would you please come up here?" Billy nodded. His heart was pounding so hard that he couldn't speak. He bent down to tie one of his shoes. Could he stuff the paper in his shoe? No, Ms. Keaton was watching him... waiting for him.

Billy glanced out the window. It was a beautiful spring day. But he wouldn't be going out for recess. He'd probably never get to go out for recess again. He swallowed hard. If only he had studied last night, instead of watching that TV show! Then, on the bus this morning, he decided to write down a few science facts on a piece of paper and hide it in the palm of his hand. It had been a crazy idea, and now he was going to pay for it.

Billy walked up slowly to Ms. Keaton's desk. In a flash, he had an idea! As he stood by her desk, he could let the paper loose from his hand and it would fall into her wastebasket. Later, he could try to get it back again. It was a great idea!

Ms. Keaton smiled at Billy. "Since you finished first," she said, "I thought you might like to help me set up our science experiment."

Billy was stunned. What luck! Ms. Keaton hadn't seen his little piece of paper. Now all he had to do was get it into the wastebasket. As he nodded, he opened his hand. The paper fluttered down. A sudden breeze from the open window pushed it as it fell. It floated right down to Ms. Keaton's feet.

"Billy, you dropped this," said Ms. Keaton. She picked it up. Then she looked at it more closely. "What exactly is this?" she asked, looking worried.

(continued on page 99)

Name _____ Date _____

Details, Details (cont.)

Mark each part of the story on page 98 as **E** for an important plot event, or **D** for a story detail.

_____ **1.** Billy watches TV instead of studying.

_____ **2.** Billy chews on his pencil.

_____ **3.** Ms. Keaton calls Billy up to her desk.

_____ **4.** Ms. Keaton smiles at Billy.

_____ **5.** Billy ties one of his shoes.

_____ **6.** Billy lets the paper fall from his hand.

_____ **7.** Billy's heart pounds.

_____ **8.** A breeze blows the paper.

_____ **9.** Ms. Keaton picks up the paper.

_____ **10.** Ms. Keaton looks at the paper.

_____ **11.** Billy thinks about recess.

_____ **12.** Ms. Keaton asks for help with the science experiment.

The story on page 98 stops at its climax. The climax is the turning point. All action in a story builds to the exciting climax. After the climax, the story usually comes to a close.

Circle the sentence you think might be the climax of a story in each example below.

13. a. Mary gives a rattle to her baby cousin.

b. Mary saves her cousin during a blizzard.

14. a. Charles Lindbergh loads a packet of sandwiches on his plane.

b. Charles Lindbergh looks down after hours of flying and finally sees land.

15. a. Little Red Riding Hood discovers her "grandmother" is really a wolf.

b. Little Red Riding Hood carries a basket decorated with flowers.

16. a. Joshua leaps out of a closet and scares his sister.

b. Joshua taps his fingers as he waits in the closet.

17. a. Josie's friends turn on the lights and yell "Surprise!"

b. Josie sees a yellow car parked near her house.

18. a. The pirates mend a sail that ripped during a storm.

b. The pirates struggle to save their ship during the storm.

When and Where

A setting tells when and where a story takes place. Read the story settings below. Describe where and when the story takes place.

1. The crowd was in an uproar. The West Bend football team had just made a field goal to tie the championship game. Both teams quickly ran off the field to get advice from their coaches. The November snow drifted down, dusting the noisy stadium with white.

When did the story take place? _____

Where did the story take place? _____

2. The stars were bright and clear. Ian and his family were gazing at the sky from the hot tub. They watched as several meteors fell. Each one made a bright trail of light across the sky.

When did the story take place? _____

Where did the story take place? _____

3. On a sunny, bright July afternoon in 1776, many people were gathering on the commons in Boston. They were getting ready for the big feast planned for the evening.

When did the story take place? _____

Where did the story take place? _____

4. The spaceship had been traveling through space for 200 years. The people on board were just coming out of stasis. They hadn't been awake since 2020. The computer was set to wake them up when the planet X59 was a week's travel away.

When did the story take place? _____

Where did the story take place? _____

Name _____ Date _____

Ralph

Ralph was a dirty mutt. His once-white hair was gray and brown with grime. He wore a black collar around his neck that had once been blue. On the dirty collar hung an identification tag, if anyone could get close enough to read it.

Right now, Ralph was on his belly. He inched forward under the lilac bushes. His long hair dragged in the dirt. His bright, black eyes were glued on a plate at the edge of the table. On it was a ham sandwich. His moist, black nose twitched with the smell. Ralph knew he would get a swat with the broom or spray with the hose if the lady of the house caught him in the yard again.

His empty belly made him brave. The screen door slammed as the lady went back for other goodies. Ralph knew it was time. He flew like a bullet to the edge of the table. The corner of the plate was in his mouth long enough to tip it onto the ground. Ralph's teeth seized the sandwich and he was off. The door slammed and a yell was heard. As he dove through a hole in the bushes, water from the hose whitened the back half of his body and his dirty tail.

1. What is Ralph? _____

Highlight in yellow details that helped you decide this.

2. Is Ralph living in a home with people the day he steals the sandwich? _____

Highlight in blue details that helped you decide this.

3. Did Ralph have a home with people at one time? _____

_____

Highlight in green details that helped you decide this.

4. How does the lady in the passage feel about Ralph? _____

What details cause you to think this? _____

_____

5. Draw Ralph in the frame above. Each time you draw a detail, highlight it in the text.

Name _____ Date _____

Classified Information

Match each genre with its definition by writing a number on each book.

1. a story about a puzzling crime

2. a true story

3. a true story about a person's life written by someone other than that person

4. a story so exaggerated it could not be true

5. a true story of a person's life by that person

6. a make-believe (not true) story

7. a verse or rhyme

8. a story about future events and future technology

9. a funny story

10. a make-believe story about a real person or a real time that existed in the past

11. a brief story that teaches a moral—often containing animal characters

12. a story about unusual characters and make-believe places

piñata

sombrero

poncho

vista

mesa

fiesta

straw or felt hat with
a wide brim and
high crown

papier mâché
object filled
with treats

a distant view seen
from a special spot

cloak with a hole in
the center for
a person's head

a festival
or celebration

high piece of land
with flat top
and steep sides

adobe

bronco

lasso

rodeo

tortilla

adiós

a wild or partly
tamed horse

straw and clay mixed
together and used
for building

a show or contest of
cowboy skills

long rope with
a sliding loop
at one end

Spanish word
for good-bye

Mexican flat
bread made
with cornmeal
or wheat flour

veterinarian

director

chef

musician

florist

physicist

a person
who guides
a business,
organization,
or actors

a doctor
for animals

a person
skilled
at music

an expert cook

a scientist
who works
with physics

a person
who works
with plants
and flowers

physician

accountant

president

editor

foreman

technician

person who checks and takes care of business records

a medical doctor

person who reads and corrects written items to be published

an officer elected to lead a group

person whose work requires special skills

leader of a group of workers in a shop, factory, or other workplace

exercise

goal

touchdown

homerun

tackle

javelin

points scored in
a sporting event

activity to keep
the body strong and
healthy

a hit that allows
a baseball batter to
touch four
bases and score

scoring six points in
football

a light spear thrown
for distance

to seize and push a
person down to stop
his progress

dribble	referee
overtime	par
pit stop	penalty

a sports official
who makes sure
players follow
the rules

to move along in
repeated bounces,
kicks, or pushes

the normal or
average amount

going beyond
the normal
time allowed

a punishment or
disadvantage given to
players who break rules

a stop for fuel
or repairs during
a car race

parallel

perpendicular

exponent

product

circumference

degree

at a right angle
to something

a plane or line
the same distance
at every point
from another

result of multiplying two
or more numbers

the written symbol in a
math problem that
shows the operation of
raising to a power

measure or amount

the distance around
something

multiply

geometry

algebra

diameter

division

quotient

area of math focused on shapes and objects

to increase the number of

a straight line that passes though the center of a circle

a form of math used to solve problems when one element is missing

the answer to a division problem

separating into parts

✂

sycamore	maple
oak	evergreen
gingko	hickory

a hardwood tree with notched leaves, grown for its sap

very large shade tree with broad oval leaves

tree with green leaves that stay on the tree all year

hardwood tree that bears acorns

hardwood tree that bears edible nuts

a shade tree with fan-shaped leaves and yellow fruit

cedar

sassafras

fir

sequoia

willow

birch

tree with both lobed
and oval good-smelling
leaves, its bark
was used
for flavoring

evergreen tree
that bears cones

huge coniferous trees
that can grow to be
over 300 feet
(90 meters)

an evergreen tree that
bears cones and
is related
to the pine

hardwood tree with
bark that easily
peels off

tree with long narrow
leaves, its twigs are
often used for weaving

0-7424-1774-3 *After School Reading Activities*

Answer Key

In Patriotic Order 6
1. *2, 1, 3   2. *2, 3, 1   3. 1, *2, 3
4. *2, 3, 1   5. *2, 3, 1   6. *2, 1, 3
7. 1, *2, 3   8. 3, *2, 1   9. *2, 1, 3
10. 3, *2, 1   11. *2, 1, 3   12. 3, *2, 1
13. *2, 1, 3   14. 1, *2, 3   15. 1, *2, 3
16. 1, *2, 3   17. 1, 3, *2   18. 1, *2, 3
19. 1, *2, 3   20. 3, *2, 1   21. 3, 1, *2
22. *2, 1, 3   23. 3, *2, 1   24. *2, 1, 3
25. *2, 1, 3   26. 3, 1, *2

They paved the way for Memorial Day.

Guide-Worthy Words 7
1. reindeer, resolute, retort, salute, schoolmaster, scowl, stance, stealth, subside, surpass
2. accidentally, accustom, additional, allow, almanac, ammunition, ancient, appoint, ashamed, assign
3. barometer, barracks, beneficial, burrow, calamity, commence, commotion, consternation, cordial, corporal
4. defiant, demoralize, discard, disposition, disturbance, earthenware, enormous, entirely, epidemic, explosive

Cloudy Skies 8
1. parties   2. dishes   3. beaches
4. ditches   5. sticks   6. lunches
7. crutches   8. pieces   9. stores
10. daisies   11. cartoons   12. dolls
13. trees   14. cherries   15. skies

Two Vowels Go Walking 9
1. ue   2. ea   3. ay   4. oa   5. ai   6. ee
7. oe   8. ay   9. ea   10. ea   11. oa   12. ai
13. oa   14. ea   15. ee   16. ai   17. ee   18. ay

What's That Noise? 10
Across
5. voyage   6. poison   7. rejoice
9. enjoy   11. appointment 13. loyalty
15. voice

Down
1. join   2. avoid   3. destroy
4. soybean   8. employer   10. moisture
12. choice   14. royal

Sweet Syllables 11
1. 3   2. 3   3. 1   4. 1   5. 2   6. 1
7. 2   8. 2   9. 3   10. 3   11. 3   12. 2
13. 3   14. 3   15. 3

The Root of the Matter 12
1. aquarium   2. portable   3. vocalist
4. biography   5. dentist   6. phonics
7. centipede   8. dormitory

Across
1. aquarium   2. phonics   3. dormitory
4. portable

Down
5. dentist   6. biography   7. vocalist
8. centipede

Break It Up! 13
1. re source ful   2. accomplish ment
3. numb ness   4. convince ing
5. mercy less   6. sturdy est
7. dis obey ing   8. un mistake able
9. dis infect ing   10. dis claim ed
11. re open ing   12. invent ive
13. rest less   14. pre caution
15. imitate ing

Let It Snow 14
Blue—2, 3, 4, 5, 7, 11, 12, 14
Red—1, 6, 8, 9, 10, 13, 15, 16, 17, 18, 19, 20

"R" Takes Charge .15
1. ar   2. or   3. ir   4. ur   5. ar   6. ur
7. er   8. ar   9. ir   10. or   11. ur   12. ar
13. or   14. er   15. ur   16. ar   17. ir   18. ir

Slippery Blasts 16
Circle the following:
blizzard, blowing, block, blow, blow, blasts, sleep, sled, sleep, sled, slip, slide, slippery. sleep, sled
Across
3. blow   5. blankets   6. slide
7. slip   8. slippery

Down
1. block   2. blizzard   3. blasts
6. sleep   7. sled

Enough! 17
cough, enough   rough
laugh, enough   tough
1. rough   2. laugh   3. tough
4. enough   5. cough

All the Way to the End 18
1. talking   2. tenderly   3. hopeful
4. folded   5. basement   6. restless, assignment
7. endlessly   8. disappointment 9. pretended
10. blazing   11. usually   12. wonderful

This Suffix Is Terrific 19
1. sporadic   2. scenic   3. scientific
4. terrific   5. volcanic   6. symphonic
7. photographic   8. Nomadic   9. romantic
10. democratic   11. angelic   12. majestic

0-7424-1774-3 After School Reading Activities

Answer Key

Fanciful Hats 20
1. raining
2. pocketful
3. motionless, motioning
4. mailing, mailer
5. mouthful, mouthing
6. roughly, roughing, rougher
7. seriously
8. basketful
9. painting, painter
10. dreamless, dreaming, dreamer
11. brighter, brightly
12. painful, painless, paining
13. working, worker
14. sweetly, sweeter
15. fasting, faster

Number Words 21
Across
2. triangle   4. unicorn   6. quadrangle
7. bifocals   8. tricycle   12. bimonthly
13. tricorn

Down
1. binoculars   2. trio   3. bicycle
5. tripod   6. quadruplet   9. unicycle
10. uniform   11. tricep

Don't Miss This 22
Base words:
adventure, apply, behave, call, cast, chance, conduct, count, deal, deed, direct, file, fire, fit, fortune, govern, guide, handle, hear, lay, lead, name, play, read, rule
1. miscast   2. mislay   3. misfortune
4. misdeal   5. misfire   6. misadventure
7. mislay   8. misread   9. misconduct
10. mislead

'Tis the Season 23
1. a   2. b   3. c   4. a   5. b   6. c
7. c   8. a   9. b   10. b   11. c   12. a

Borrowed from Abroad 24
1. [middle Dutch] a small tool to bore holes
2. [Spanish] a large estate or ranch, or the main house on one
3. [middle French] a light spear used in an athletic event
4. [Spanish] dried meat strips
5. [French] a place where dead bodies are kept
6. [Italian] flooring made of marble chips and set in cement, then polished
7. hacienda and jerky
8. morgue and javelin
9. jerky
10. hacienda

Similar in Some Way 25
1. director is to play   2. adult is to child
3. zipper is to skirt   4. beef is to cattle
5. alter is to change   6. scissors is to cut
7. convince is to persuade   8. Halloween is to holiday
9. trousers is to cuffs   10. cereal is to breakfast
11. explore is to investigate

Aardvark to Zebra .26
1. aardvark   2. rabbit   3. raccoon
4. hidden   5. cheetah   6. stuffing
7. egg   8. hitchhike   9. skiing
10. shell   11. hammer   12. funny
13. cookie   14. hippo   15. sorry
16. crossword   17. shuttle   18. vacuum
19. drizzle

Hear! Here! for Homophones 27
1. heel, heal, he'll   2. paced, paste
3. please, pleas   4. crew's, cruise
5. bolder, boulder   6. muscle, mussel
7. pare, pear   8. peeks, peaks
9. Wait, weight   10. colonel, kernel
11–15. Sentences will vary.

This Will Be No Contest for You 28
1. (k ə n tent), (kan tent)   2. (cloz), (clos)
3. (k ə n test), (kan test)   4. (di zurt), (dez ə rt)
5. (ri kord), (rek ə rd)   6. (k ə myoon), (kam yoon)
7. (ri fyooz), (ref yoos)   8. (es kort), (i skort)

Your Number's Up .29
1. Pentagon   2. octopus   3. biathlon
4. bilingual   5. quadrupeds   6. hexagon
7. centennial   8. trisect   9. centipede
10. trio   11. unicorn   12. decade
13. quadrilateral   14. decathlon

Now Try This 30
1. tricycle   2. tricolored   3. trivet
4. triceratops   5. tricentennial   6. tripod
7. triple   8. triplets   9. trifocal
10. triceps   11. triplicate   12. trio
13. trilogy   14. triangle   15. trident

Forests 31
Across
3. conservation   5. pulp   6. plywood
8. tree farm   9. fertilizer

Down
1. forest ranger   2. millpond   4. sawmill
7. logger   8. tropical

0-7424-1774-3 *After School Reading Activities*

Answer Key

Weird Words **32**
1. gargle   2. epitaph   3. calliope
4. gargoyle   5. bamboozle   6. calligraphy
7. barcarole   8. cajolery   9. argyles
10. gondola

Geographic Juggle **33**
1. valley   2. mountain   3. canyon
4. volcano   5. harbor   6. plain
7. ocean   8. coast   9. river
10. peninsula   11. gulf   12. continent
13. sea   14. plateau   15. island
16. lake

Don't Pollute **34**
Across
1. erosion   6. oil spill   8. ecology
10. environment

Down
2. radiation   3. smog   4. pollution
5. recycle   7. pesticides   9. litter

Birds of a Feather **35**
Answers may vary.

Some Body **36**
1. brain   2. lungs   3. liver
4. heart   5. kidneys   6. stomach
7. heart   8. stomach   9. lungs
10. brain   11. kidneys   12. liver

Threatened and Endangered Animals **37**
1. dugong   2. gavial   3. Darwin's rhea

Antonyms from A to Z **40**
Across
5. kind   7. peril   8. urge
10. able   11. evade   12. meager
13. grief   18. console   20. seize
22. vain   23. jolly   24. warm
25. betray

Down
1. repel   2. liberal   3. quiet
4. defend   6. near   9. fatigue
14. insult   15. young   16. honor
17. tense   19. odd   21. zany

Football Fame Frames **41**
Super Bowl

Medieval March **42**
Across
1. chivalry   2. Excalibur   3. round table
5. joust   6. Merlin   7. lance
8. moat   9. vassal   10. tournament

Down
1. squire   2. page   3. cathedral
4. knight   5. armor   6. monastery
7. friar   8. coat of arms   9. castle

Eating Dessert in the Desert **44**
1. breath   2. lie   3. picture
4. lose   5. accept   6. dessert
7. lay   8. sit   9. except
10. set   11. pitcher   12. breathe
13. loose   14. desert

About the Book **45**
1. author   2. theme   3. character
4. dialogue   5. climax   6. antagonist
7. protagonist   8. setting   9. illustrations
10. plot   11. conflict   12. conclusion

Shortcuts **46**
1. e   2. g   3. n   4. I   5. l   6. a
7. k   8. b   9. c   10. j   11. d   12. f
13. o   14. h   15. m

La Fiesta **47–48**
Across
4. vista   5. banana   7. chocolate
9. rodeo   10. patio   13. canyon
15. mosquito   16. salsa   17. tortilla

Down
1. bronco   2. tambourine   3. Santa Fe
4. vanilla   6. lasso   8. poncho
11. taco   12. piñata   14. guitar
15. mesa

Sensory Words **49**
Some answers may vary.
Taste: sweet, bitter, sour, salty

Hear: singing, talking, mooing, barking

Smell: smoky, piney, dusty, moldy

See: raindrop, books, red, butterfly

Code Names **50**
1. cage   2. cheap   3. correct   4. carry
5. core   6. copy   7. coop   8. chart
9. chat   10. cheer   11. crop   12. creep
13. care   14. catch   15. category   16. charge
17. cohere   18. coerce   19. chore   20. cheat

Compound Fun **53**
1. butterfly   2. honeycomb   3. horseshoe
4. quarterback   5. skateboard   6. skyscraper
7. toadstool   8. turtleneck

0-7424-1774-3 *After School Reading Activities*

Answer Key

The Mystery of a Secret Code 56
1. clues   2. suspense   3. alibi
4. confession   5. evidence   6. deduction
7. witness   8. suspects
9. Watch out for the red herrings! They are false clues.

Compute-a-Word .57
Words will vary.

Two Words in One 58
1. hairspray   2. peanut butter   3. flowerbed
4. catfish   5. pancake   6. eyeball
7. tree house   8. eardrum   9. doorbell
10. basketball   11. rainbow   12. handbag

Holiday Happenings 59
1. New Year's Day   2. Martin Luther King, Jr. Day
3. Groundhog Day   4. Valentine's Day
5. St. Patrick's Day   6. April Fool's Day
7. Mother's Day   8. Memorial Day
9. Father's Day   10. Independence Day
11. Labor Day   12. Columbus Day
13. Halloween   14. Thanksgiving
15. Christmas (may alternate with 16)
16. Hanukkah (may alternate with 15)

Palindrome Pals .60
1. pup   2. noon   3. level   4. peep
5. repaper   6. toot   7. bob   8. eve
9. solos   10. gig   11. Dad   12. radar
13. race car   14. deed   15. ewe   16. tot
17. gag   18. sis   19. wow   20. eye

From Whose Point of View? 61
Sentences may vary.

Bugs Are Good for You 62–63
1. Some people eat insects for nutritional value and taste.
2. Some insects have high nutritional value.
3. Some people eat insects because they taste great.
4. People from other parts of the world may think
   we eat strange things.

Deep in the Earth 64–65
1. rocks
2. Rocks are formed in three ways.
3. Topic Sentence: There are three kinds of rocks.

Subtopics: igneous rock, sedimentary rock,
metamorphic rock

Supporting Details: Igneous rocks are formed deep inside
the earth's core; when lava cools, it forms igneous rocks.
Sedimentary rock is made up of loose materials in water
that dissolve and then get cemented together.
Metamorphic rocks are formed by a major change; it
may even change its mineral makeup.

Find the Effect .68
1. e   2. a   3. f   4. d   5. c   6. b

If—Then 69
1. f   2. s   3. k   4. a   5. q   6. o
7. h   8. t   9. m   10. b   11. p   12. j
13. u   14. g   15. d   16. r   17. i   18. c
19. l   20. e   21. n

The Greatest Gift 70–71
1. She had an unusual style.
2. He wanted to give it to Grandpa for his birthday.
3. The photos were torn and faded.
4. Her painting brought the past back to him and showed
   him how special many people had been in his life.

Make It 72
2, 4, 3, 1   3, 1, 4, 2
4, 2, 1, 3   1, 4, 2, 3

Putting It All Together 73
1. Snap the table legs into the tabletop; this is number 2,
   and number 2 is the second step.
2. Before; this is number 3, and the step for screwing in the
   small screws is number 4.
3. Possible answer: If all the pieces are not there and she
   begins, she will spend time on work that she cannot
   finish. She might put the screws into two cups.
4. Answers will vary, but each paragraph should include a
   topic sentence and should tell the steps in the correct
   order. They should include the time/order words from the
   question.

Right Back at You 74
1. To give you information about bats; reasons will vary, but
   should show that the author gave facts.
2. Answers will vary, but should show a primary purpose of
   informing, not persuading, entertaining, or expressing
   feelings.

The Soldier's Lucky Coin 75–76
1. Fact—because the coin was found.
2. Yes. The special message that had been on Dixon's coin
   was on this coin.
3. b
4. Possible answer: The author is not trying to make the
   reader do anything. The events in the passage really
   happened, so the passage is not fiction. The passage is
   not mostly about feelings and can be entertaining.
5. Answers will vary, but the purpose of the first passage
   should be to give information.

An "Egg"citing Discovery 77
1. a. dinosaur   3. Answers will vary.
2. a. very old
   b. reptile
   c. not extinct

                    0-7424-1774-3 *After School Reading Activities*

Answer Key

Big Dreams 78–79
1. He wouldn't be able to enter his own store when he became an adult.
2. He mentions wearing a seat belt.
3. motivated, enthusiastic, excited
4. Answers will vary.
5. The toy store will be larger than a football field. Children would probably enjoy playing in his store.
6. Answers will vary.

How a Mosquito Bites 80–81
1. malaria, yellow fever
2. hot, moist lands near the equator
3. They don't bite, they stab and sip the blood.
4. The proboscis sips like a straw.
5. Most of us are allergic to mosquito saliva, which is left under the skin.
6. She needs blood for egg development.
7. Mosquitoes eat plant juice.

My First Job, Part One 82–83
Answers may vary:
1. Cassie is a young girl on her first baby-sitting job. She is confident, determined, and a hard worker.
2. Bart is a young and mischievous child who causes trouble for Cassie.
3. a. He put his hand in the chocolate pudding
   b. He throws the spaghetti
   c. tracks spaghetti through the house

My First Job, Part Two 84–85
1. Answers may vary:
   a. He dumps the bubble bath into the tub.
   b. He kicks blocks all over the room.
2. 4, 2, 1, 5, 3

Jumping to Conclusions 86
Answers will vary.

Scrambled Words .87
1. appeal
2. cactus
3. comet
4. exhale
5. funnel
6. magic
7. single
8. adobe
9. vanilla
10. simply
11. linen
12. hungry
13. success
14. factory
15. hiccups

Look for the Clues 88
1. rest
2. generously gives
3. annoyed
4. dresser
5. best
6. returned
7. necessary
8. friendly

A Class of Its Own 89
1. Birds, snake
2. School Subjects, movie
3. Small Fruits, watermelon
4. Dog Breeds, lion
5. Flowers, pink
6. State Names, Chicago
Answers will vary.

Similes Are Like 90
1. snow
2. the moon
3. a star
4. a bear
5. an ox
6. a rock
7. molasses
8. a deer
9. popsicle, ice
10. dough, clay
11. clown, hyena

Is That True? 91
1. NF, F
2. F, NF
3. NF, F
4. NF, F
5. F, NF
6. NF, F
7. F, NF

Football and Soccer 92
Football: oval ball, US and Canada, 110 m x 49 m field, players wear protective gear, touchdowns = 6 pts., players run or pass ball

Both: two teams, 11 players, starts with kickoff

Soccer: round ball, players kick or head ball, players wear shin guards, goals are 1 point, played all over world, field 91–119 meters long and 46–91 meters wide

The White House Gang 93–94
1. The Roosevelt children had fun living in the White House.
2. The White House gang got into mischief at the White House.
3. Answers will vary.
4. One child rode a pony upstairs. The children spit paper balls at Jackson's picture. They declared war on the White House.
5–6. Answers will vary.
7. parrot, bear, lizard, rooster, barn owl, rabbit, pig, pony
8. Answers will vary.
9. He asked for peace through his war department.
10–12. Answers will vary.

A Big, Hairy Spider 95–96
1. tarantula
2. bite you
3. feel a bite like a bee sting
4. A tarantula might jump on it, bite it, and eat it.
5. A person might get bitten; a person might get tiny tarantula hairs on her skin or eyes.
6. a tarantula
7. get bitten by a tarantula
8. Answers will vary.
9. It might die.
10. You might get tarantula hairs in your eyes or in other parts of your body; or you might get bitten.
11. The tarantula got its name from a big wolf spider that lives near Taranto, Italy.
12. A disease contracted from the wolf spider that makes a person jump in the air and make loud noises.

0-7424-1774-3 *After School Reading Activities*

Answer Key

Two Friends, Two Problems **97**
1. Ralph: his aunt's house; Sheila: her grandmother's house
2. Ralph: too much work; Sheila: too little to do
3. Ralph: tired; Sheila: bored
4. Both: going back to school

Details, Details **98–99**
1. E	2. D	3. E	4. D	5. D	6. E
7. D	8. E	9. E	10. E	11. D	12. E
13. b.	14. b.	15. a.	16. a.	17. a.	18. b.

When and Where **100**
1. When: November
   Where: football field
2. When: evening
   Where: outside under the stars
3. When: afternoon in July 1776
   Where: in the common area in Boston
4. When: in the future
   Where: in a spaceship

Ralph **101**
1. Ralph is a dog.
2. No; he is dirty and hungry.
3. Yes; he has a collar.
4. She does not like Ralph; she has swatted him with a broom and sprayed him with a hose before.
5. Drawings will vary, but should show a dirty dog with very long hair.

Classified Information **102**
1. mystery
2. nonfiction
3. biography
4. tall tale
5. autobiography
6. fiction
7. poetry
8. science fiction
9. humor
10. historical fiction
11. fable
12. fantasy

0-7424-1774-3 *After School Reading Activities*